MW01137174

Live Your Best Retirement. Your Life Depends On It

Have a Fun and Fearless Retirement with the Help of Authentic Lessons That Go Beyond Finances

Ramon C Reid

the use of the information contained within this document, including, but not limited to, errors, omissions, or inaccuracies.

Table of Contents

Preface

During my early days of retirement I was often asked questions by friends and acquaintances approaching their third age. Questions like:

- How do you fill your day?

- How come you seem so busy – you're retired?

- Shouldn't you be relaxing more?

- Why do you look healthier now than when you were working and younger?

I also noticed a worrying trend in people who had retired. A lot were lost and unfocussed or even worse they seemed angry that retirement hadn't delivered the goods. They weren't as happy as they thought they should be and they didn't know why? Even worse, they didn't know what to do about it.

This was not a problem for me nor my wife. And we're not alone as many others seem to have found the formula for a happy, healthy and fulfilling retirement.

I was curious however to find out what was going on and why. What started off as notes of discussions and research into the topic expanded. One day I thought it may benefit others to read some of what I learned during the process and the idea for this book came to be. It is a collection of thoughts and reflections on what I believe are the more critical areas to explore if you want a great retirement ... or life for that matter.

I thank my family and the friends and acquaintances I interrogated for their patience during this time. I enjoyed the process and hope that the content is useful to others considering retirement or those discovering there are some gaps in what they expected.

Enjoy the book and take from it what you need. Explore options and ideas.

Go and live your best life. Enjoy your journey, shaping it along the way.

Ramon C Reid

Introduction

The biggest fear keeping people over 55 awake at night is that their savings will run out before they do. The macabre thought may explain the obsession with financial planning in retirement circles, often at the expense of other equally weighty topics (Hoyt, 2022).

For size, consider that an estimated 10,000 Americans will turn 65 each day for the next two decades. That means almost 73 million seniors will join the ranks of older people by 2042, a trend that will have enormous implications for both the retirement sector and indeed the U.S. economy (Vandenbroucke, 2019).

Clearly, it's time to pay close attention to the factors that will shape your retirement. By not addressing those elements, you run the risk of losing not just your precious money but missing out on your retirement dream.

It's astounding how some people put more effort into planning a dinner party for 20 people than thinking about the next 20 years of their lives. The Hail Mary approach, that "it'll all work out," clearly counts for more in some people's minds than a thorough examination of some of the pressing issues and real concerns weighing on their future.

Part of the problem is our human nature. It's a trait the media plugs into seamlessly by skimping on a rational appraisal of what lies ahead and fixating on a possible future full of fear.

Psychology of Fear

The psychology of fear runs deep through the human psyche, all the way back to our cave-dwelling ancestors and their daily struggle for survival.

Those fears continue to haunt modern humankind and bedevil our clumsy efforts to make sense of an increasingly turbulent world. Our contemporary landscape may be more advanced, developed, and refined, but the threats to our human existence are no less existential. Lest we forget, the human species is at the mercy of pandemics, climate change, and nuclear war, all dangers lurking on the horizon.

Much of our anxiety is brought on by our insecurities and a fear of the unknown. The uncertainty spawns demons of its own that tend to mess with our endeavors to build a secure life with the years we have left on Earth.

People approach retirement very differently. Complicating things even more is the retirement industry itself, a hugely complex, layered behemoth that spans housing, insurance, medical facilities, and care. Total U.S. retirement assets alone amount to an eye-watering $33.7 trillion (Quarterly Retirement Market Data, 2022).

Not surprisingly, the composition and complexion of retirement sectors across the developed world is remarkably similar. The practical choices facing older people planning for their retirement clearly count for plenty. But should a tick box of facilities be the only determinant of your retirement? What if some of the ticks you want are not listed? What if you tick the wrong box? Or if the box you do tick, you no longer want?

Dilemma of Planning in the Dark

At root is an intractable dilemma facing seniors—having to make decisions about the future based on what you know today. Life has a habit of happening, sometimes in sync with your planning, and other times, it throws you a nasty curveball from the outfield.

All change, no matter how dramatic or otherwise, is disruptive. Your life of leisure expectations may not have panned out, your retirement destination no longer appeals, or a life partner's sudden death has upended your carefully structured two-year plan. Chances are these events catch you unawares.

Three very different case studies illustrate the vagaries of life that highlight an incontestable truth—the only constant in life is change.

Jim and Judy: A Considered Adventure

Jim and Judy, both career-chartered accountants with a multinational consultancy, worked and resided in cities across the world. They lived life to the fullest and experienced some envious bucket-list adventures. As gregarious and astute expats, they had the world at their feet.

Imagine the surprise when I heard they had invested in an "Over-50s Lifestyle Village." Wouldn't that cramp their lifestyle, I wondered.

Their answer was both surprising and delightfully coherent. It was a considered decision that suited their needs, they said as they counted off the points:

- They like the community.

- They moved into a ready-made community.

- They are close to the golf club and gym.

- They want the convenience of a "lock-and-go" unit to

  - downsize

  - free up extra cash

  - reduce upkeep time and costs

  - improve security

  - travel and pursue adventure and activities.

Jim and Judy certainly ticked all the boxes, and then some, especially blending their lust for life with their new reality.

It was, as the cliche goes, a win-win scenario all round when stacked up against the principles of a liberating philosophy, that of positive psychology. More about the pioneering work of psychologist Martin Seligman later, but suffice to point out that at this stage that Jim and Judy were

- clear and optimistic about their future

- deeply engaged in making it happen

- ready to chase their passion for travel and exploration

- while not neglecting relationships.

Brad and Patty: Wisdom Wanting

Brad and Patty have a different story. Diligent and hardworking all their lives, they prudently saved for retirement. When the time came, they bought a wonderful beachfront property in their favorite holiday town.

The idea was that friends, and especially family, would love to visit. But their reasoning was way out of kilter as far as their hopes for retirement were concerned. With the benefit of hindsight, it's fair to observe that

- they are not sociable

- have no outside interests

- struggled to make friends

- have nothing to replace the passing "booze and cruise" phase

- the town is too remote for regular visitors.

The upshot is that they are more or less homebound looking after a demanding property in the forlorn hope of visitors. Instead of enjoying the stunning beachside environment they have chosen, Brad and Patty limit their outings to buying groceries and paying utility bills.

They are having second thoughts about the wisdom of their choices and realize something has to change. But they have no idea what to do or where to start.

It's fair to observe that Brad and Patty were

- missing out on relationships

- lacking in engaging activities

- struggling for meaning once the party period was over

- experiencing very little satisfaction.

Ray and Collette: Pragmatic Progress

My wife and I opted for a more pragmatic approach around our decision to retire early. Our path was motivated by a number of key factors because we

- love our new property

- have a number of key projects in mind

- are active physically as keen gardeners, cyclists, and kayakers

- are emotionally centered with regular meetups with friends and family

- are intellectually stimulated as part time business and management consultants, performing coaching, and personal training.

We chose a retirement route that matched our needs without compromising the structures and routines that governed most of our lives. We made purposeful decisions about how we wanted to live our third age.

Six years later after our first tentative steps, things keep on getting better. Key is being able to review, refresh, and redesign aspects of it.

What It All Means

Whatever you do, don't allow retirement to just happen. Going with the flow and spontaneity has its place in life but not in the planning of your final earthly trimester.

You want to craft a plan that celebrates the fundamentals of a good life. People have different priorities, so go figure which qualities in your life rank highest.

Take your time, chew over your options, do some navel-gazing. Listen to your heart and head in equal measure. Write and rewrite lists, read, research, and then some. Speak to people who are also thinking about retirement and those who are retired. Don't limit your questions to people you know. Don't be shy to seek counsel from people outside your usual circle. You never know, you may come across something entirely new or perhaps have your feelings confirmed.

If you're unsure about what you want to do in retirement, start experimenting with new activities. A passion, or even an abiding interest, doesn't just show up; you've got to find them.

Don't fret about what you don't know. Plan for what you do know, draw up budgets, add an overestimated annual inflation number, and see if the math works out.

If you're downscaling, compare the specifications of the two new retirement villages going up against an existing facility. Also weigh up the pros and cons of moving into a smaller unit in your town against moving somewhere else.

Trust your financial plans. You have earned the right to start thinking beyond the mere numbers, knowing that a change in direction doesn't need to mean a crippling outflow of funds. You want to embrace retirement with the confidence and enthusiasm it deserves.

Retirement, after all, is not about withdrawing from your life. It's about remodeling your life to match your needs and desires. Remember, you'll be retired for between 20 and 30 years based on life expectancy data. Start thinking about what kind of retirement you want for yourself, tease out some of the suggestions. The ideas below may be helpful:

- Actively take control: Make a conscious decision for a disciplined planning approach. Be systematic and thorough. Assessing your finances is a sensible start.

- Explore options and ideas.

- Build on them, test them out.

  o If you dream of retiring to a remote mountain hamlet, spend at least two weeks there. You will know soon enough if your happy holiday is the same as a permanent stay.

Above all, make it your goal to flourish, not just exist in retirement. As we're about to see, "to flourish" is a key theme in designing your ideal retirement status.

Holy Grail of Retiring

While you want to get the big ticket items right in retirement, you will need a healthy dose of flexibility in your planning. Life happens, and sometimes the things you can't control mess up your carefully laid out plans.

Your wherewithal to absorb the unexpected shockwaves—big and small—will strengthen your resilience to adapt to changing circumstances.

A Personal Philosophy

Our initial foray into early retirement was predicated on a life of happiness we envisioned for ourselves. Later, to our delight, we discovered that our intuitive thinking harmonized with the philosophy of the school of positive psychology and the pioneering work of American psychologist Dr Martin Seligman.

A nutshell definition of positive psychology says it all: "The study of what constitutes the pleasant life, the engaged life, and the meaningful life" (Ackerman, 2019).

At the core of Seligman's evidence-based work on improving people's quality of life is the concept of 'flourishing,' which is founded on six elements of the PERMA-V model:

- positive emotions

- engagement

- relationships

- meaning

- accomplishments

- vitality.

By including vitality, or the V, to the PERMA model, Seligman pretty much laid down the spine of our quest for a remarkable retirement.

This framework of positivity is a massive thumbs-up for joy and contentment in life, by far the most important quest in our golden years.

It's pleasing to note that the positive roles of these attributes are validated in numerous studies on aging, longevity, health, happiness, and quality of life drawn from experiences across the world (Crowfoot, 2022).

This book provides insights that can turn the power of positive action into a pathway for you to create the joyful and healthy retirement life you want. I look forward to walking the journey of exploration and discovery with you!

Chapter 1:

The Pain of Redundancy

There's no way of softening the blow of redundancy and retrenchment. It's a professional slap in the face that catches you by surprise and leaves you in shock.

It's a horribly familiar scenario for countless people in their fifties whose plans for a structured retirement plan are torn up and thrown into the wind.

The call that upends lives comes when least expected. Loyalty doesn't count for much when it comes to culling the head count.

No matter how the news is sugar-coated, it can't hide the brutal truth—being forced to stop work before you had planned to.

The initial shock is only the first rapid of the white-knuckle ride down a torrent of emotions. Anger, resentment, rage, and a sense of helplessness overcome you, so much so you start doubting your own sanity.

Sunken Dreams

One of the saddest stories is that of Brian, a welding foreman and keen fisherman who was looking forward to living out his twilight years on a piece of land bordering a lake. For more than 15 years, Brian had been sinking every cent into his dream property, paying off the mortgage, and building it up and adding value.

Then his daughter fell critically ill, and he took out a mortgage to pay for the six-month stay in hospital.

Not a year later, Brian was summoned to the office. Thank you for the 36 years of service, he was told, we'd decided to bring in younger blood. You can keep the welder, his boss said, consider it a severance gift.

Without the wage to keep up payments, Brian had no choice but to sell his property. At the age of 58, Brian had lost his entire investment and his dream. All he had to look forward to was a modest pension pay-out. Worst was the blow to his sense of self-worth, a setback he never fully recovered from.

Triumph of the Human Spirit

The good news is that not all retrenchment stories end in doom and gloom. If anything, the trove of accounts that celebrate achievement over adversity is surprisingly plentiful and popular.

These remarkable stories are about people staring down the fear of retirement and winning. These accounts brim with lessons and insights, thoughts, ideas, perspectives, and possibilities that show just how resilient the human spirit is.

It's the kind of attitude that says that if life throws you a lemon, make a glass of sparkling lemonade. In the case of a go-getting career woman being dumped from her workplace, she didn't let the grass grow under her feet and turned pasture into paradise.

Margery: Morphing Miracle

Margery was a C-suite executive in a government entity that helped smooth the implementation of policy. It was a high-powered job that made plenty of demands on Margery. At least she was able to count on the support of her husband and family.

Then the axe fell. A new political administration made good on its election promise of cutting public sector costs and promptly did away with her entire department. With the stroke of a pen, Margery and her colleagues were deemed "supernumerary to the needs of the government" and summarily retrenched.

She did not expect the blow, not after a stellar 15-year career with her sights set on a departmental directorship. Marge took the blow personally. If the ease of dismissal made her angry, the disdain for her leadership of a hard-working unit plunged her into a deep depression.

Adding insult to injury, Marge was a healthy, ambitious 63-year-old woman with two degrees and an MBA who was not ready to put up her feet and sip cocktails all day. These preoccupations weighed on Marge and her worried friends who walked on egg-shells around her.

The tide finally turned when we cracked the nod to an early dinner for "an announcement." The spectacular balcony setting and beautifully presented table gave away the game—a dry run for the new chapter in the lives of Marge and husband Corin.

They realized after much soul-searching and navel-gazing that a possible future had stared them in the face all along—their life-long passion for fine food and wine. Already held in high esteem for their knowledge and culinary prowess, Marge and Corin effortlessly pivoted their new life toward judging both food and wine.

It was an inspired move that opened doors they didn't know existed. A tentative food and wine pairing course was a riotous success that was booked out months ahead. At least once every two months, they're jetting off somewhere to judge or taste at an event.

Their new life has also given them the time and space to pursue other dreams, like finally moving to a quaint hamlet in the heart of the Chenin-wine growing region. As if to validate their life change, Marge and Corin are looking forward to becoming grandparents to twins in less than six months.

Drawing on the PERMA-V model, it's clear that Marge and Corin had found new meaning and a sense of achievement in their new life. Life certainly was more engaging, and they're constantly making meaningful connections with like-minded people.

Marvelous Magic

Marge still marvels at what she calls the magic, how the threat of adversity morphed into a life beyond expectations. The trick behind the transition? Doing her darndest not to let the changes out of her control affect what she could control.

Margery's story was plenty of food for thought among her friends. We laughed and joked about the magical morphing miracle but agreed that Marge was, well, unshakably Marge. The disciplined and methodical ethos of her previous corporate world lives on but tempered by the joy of living life in the present.

For fun, we mapped Marge's magical morphing miracle. This is what we came up with.

How to Handle a Sinkhole

There's no advance warning for a sinkhole. A crater opens and swallows you. This is what happened to Marge when she was retrenched. She found herself in a bad place. Then her survival instincts kicked in and she

1. climbed out of the hole

2. called on the support of her family and friends

3. thought long and hard about her choices

4. plugged into her tough-as-teak work ethos

5. grooved into an obvious solution

6. interrogated the ideas

7. tested the concepts

8. piloted the project.

Clouds of Uncertainty

Not everybody is as methodical and go-getting as Margery, we agreed. For some, the prospect of retirement is daunting enough of a trial. Having to deal with the crisis of redundancy or retrenchment is downright terrifying.

Best then, we agreed, was to plan for retirement and be prepared for retrenchment. That takes some doing. Does that mean a Plan B in case Plan A crashes? Or does it mean one plan to accommodate both the retirement and redundancy scenarios?

We also agreed that the only difference is that retirement is voluntary, and retrenchment is not. In both cases, uncertainty about what lies ahead clouds the horizon. Some of the elements waiting in the "new normal" are

- more choices about most aspects in your life

- more time on your hands

- feelings of restlessness and lethargy

- elevated levels of anxiety

- fears about your financial security.

Plan Ahead

The only way out of the fog is to plan ahead. Plans may change; that's the nature of planning. It's not an event, it's a process.

Drawing up a list, even creating spreadsheets, will help to focus the mind and channel your thoughts. Perhaps think along these lines below:

- What gives you pleasure?

- What don't you like?

- What are your dreams?

- Can your finances fund your wishes?

- What have you always wanted to do but never had time or the opportunity?

- Write a separate bucket list of things to do.

  - Don't confuse a bucket list with a passion. You may fantasize about landing a marlin, but that doesn't necessarily mean you love angling enough to buy a deep-sea fishing boat.

Possibilities and Opportunities

The idea is to create a mindmap of the possibilities and opportunities open to you. None of these ideas are written in stone, but they help sketch a vision of what you want for yourself.

You don't want to drift aimlessly in a sea of indecision. You want to set your compass on a course for the future. Navigating the future is easier if you

- are able to retire and not be retrenched

- are prepared for more than one option

- learn fast or can adapt

- look forward to the future with excitement and not look back in grief

- can imagine a new future

- review your plans from time to time.

Chapter 2:

Effective Planning

Who would have thought that the buyer of our dear friends' house would become our very good friend? The odd thing was that Hank and Liz Franklin, the sellers, and the buyer, Jock, sold and bought the same house for the same reason—retirement.

After almost 40 years owning a busy pharmacy, the Franklins decided to move closer to their daughter and her family, three time zones away. They want to watch their grandchildren grow up before their twilight years become too dark to see, they joked at the time.

A lightning quick sale, before being listed, of their wonderful home high up on a ridge overlooking the ocean turbocharged their retirement plans.

We were delighted for Hank and Liz but sad at the shock loss of our friends. More surprising was that the buyer was from out-of-town. How did he know about the property?

All was revealed when we met Jock at the farewell party for the Franklins. He had been visiting the area for two years and liked what he had seen. He asked all three real estate agencies to let him know when a property was for sale. Before word was out about our friend's home, Jock had already made a generous offer.

Hank and Liz accepted, and in one fell swoop, two retirement deals were struck. On the face of things, it seemed like a win-win scenario. In reality, it panned out a little different. While Jock thrived, our friends found themselves out of sorts.

Devil in the Detail

On reflection, the different outcomes can be traced to the opposite approaches by Jock and our friends to retirement. While Jock was meticulous and methodical, our beloved friends were a lot more vague and a lot less focused. Clearly a case of the "devil is in the detail" that Jock got right and the Franklins not so much.

Jock: Finding His Place

Jock may be the new owner of our old friends' house, but he was also deeply respectful of the community he had chosen to retire in. Single in his early sixties after electing not to remarry following the tragic death of his wife and two children in a car crash 30 years ago, Jock was a bit of an anomaly.

He made up for his single marital status with an infectious passion for the ocean. As a retired marine biologist with a deep interest in ocean conservation, Jock brought new energy to the community. Never overbearing, Jock shared his knowledge with people who showed interest.

His guided early morning beach walks became a must-do activity as did the occasional evening session on the terrace with its 180-degree view of the ocean.

Sunset was Jock's favorite time of the day. In a routine that soon became familiar and guests were expected to join, he would raise his glass to the end of "another day in glorious paradise."

It's a charming, sincere ritual we've come to respect Jock for. One evening, after an enthralling display by a pod of humpback whales on their migratory route, I asked Jock about the sunset soiree.

"Well," he smiled, "it's my daily prompt never to take anything for granted, especially not at the gates of paradise."

It was a lesson in humility, respect, and above all, about paying gracious tribute to the community that had welcomed him. Being accepted, no, welcomed, sealed the success of Jock's planning.

In the parlance of the PERMA-V structure, Jock radiates positivity, pursues meaningful engagement, and is building great relationships. Little wonder he is thriving and brimming with vitality.

Hank and Lyn Franklin: Ground Zero Reset

New life for the Franklins started off on a rocky footing. They moved to a rented apartment on the top floor of a complex overlooking a suburban park in a mid-sized town they had visited three times before.

The reason for each visit was to see their daughter, her new husband, and their six-month-old granddaughter. The happy visits to the largeish town persuaded them that retiring in the same town would be the answer. They would be closer to the family, would downscale, and would be able to build a new life there.

The culture shock hit them in their third week. The apartment was claustrophobic, the view dull, and the town uninspiring. Worse, they had only seen their daughter's family three times. The reason for the move was not panning out so well.

Real life for a starter family with both parents keeping down full-time jobs was tough. There simply wasn't any free time, as Hank and Lyn had assumed. The only practical meeting time was over a weekend. Even then, there were competing interests.

Reality dawned that they were only part players in their children's lives. They had projected their wishes on the lives of people they had no control over. Not a good start for what should have been a rigorous interrogation.

The only way of the flawed state of affairs was ground zero of the decision-making process. To get out of the hole they had dug themselves, they decided on a few measures.

- They offered to babysit their granddaughter for three months.

- The gesture was deeply appreciated by their cash-strapped daughter and son-in-law.

- They built relationships with all three members of their family.

- They bought time to reconsider plans for the future.

• They realized they weren't ready for a passive retirement.

• They choose to travel, a dream long deferred while working.

• They bought an RV and hit the road, literally.

Their galivanting for the foreseeable future effectively pushed the pause button on their final retirement plans. But, as we came to realize, their travels were merely the next chapter in their retirement story.

It does raise the question whether our friends got things wrong, or was it just their way of doing things? It sure is a journey unlike most other twilight adventures but a path that suited their lifestyle.

Comparing Notes

The vastly different experiences of Jock and the Franklins can be narrowed down to a single factor—planning. It's uncanny how everything that Jock had done, our friends did the opposite. For fun, Colette and I compared the planning elements as they pertained to our new and old friends.

Planning Element	Jock	PERMA-V
Research	Investigated town for two years	Engaged
Social sensitivity	Studied social dynamics	Meaning
Status awareness	Aware of outsider status	Relationships
Service and value	Maritime interests fitted with town's overall value	Passion
Primed and ready	Put estate agencies on notice to buy, arranged finances in advance	Achievement
Commitment	Struck deal with irresistible offer	Vitality

Planning Element	Hank and Lyn	PERMA-V
Research	Three visits to town	n/a

Social sensitivity	No knowledge	n/a
Status awareness	No regard	n/a
Service and value	No contribution	n/a
Primed and ready	Renting apartment was a stop-gap measure	n/a
Commitment	Committing only to a 6-month lease	n/a

Beating About the Bush

The experiences of two acquaintances from the university city, about two hours away, illustrate a similar point. Sol, the managing director of a very successful family retail business, handed over the reins to the two sons.

He was excited by the generational hand-over. After almost 30 years, Sol was ready to hand over the day-to-day drudgery. He would be available for consultation and giving advice on significant matters affecting the business.

His wife was in full support of his decision to retire early. She thoroughly enjoyed her work as a lecturer at the university and resolved to cut her commitments by about half.

Being financially well off, their plan was to do more traveling. But Covid and its restrictions put paid to their plans.

Suddenly Sol found himself in limbo. His plans didn't pan out, and he had too many hours in the day. He joined a golf club, took up fishing, and took on various "projects of interest."

However, none of these activities really excited or gave him joy. His day was filled with a series of tasks, even chores, that gave him no pleasure. Slowly, the spring in his step disappeared, and he gradually fell into longer periods of silence and depression.

This he kept to himself until an unexpected breakdown revealed the depth of his depression. Sol found the rapid shift from a busy day to hours of emptiness too much. It left him with a sense of worthlessness, or a pointless existence, in which he had no place.

A Picture Telling the Story

By contrast, Sol's accountant friend Garth had a much happier landing under similar circumstances. He sold his shares in the accountancy practice he had built with the aim to retire early and pursue his passion for adventure riding.

His wife, a matron at a private hospital, supported the idea, mainly because she hoped the change would be good for his worryingly high blood pressure.

Garth grooved into retirement as smooth as the take-off on his motorbike. Most weekends, he goes on an outride, and on weekdays he plays golf and racket-ball with friends and former colleagues.

A weekly chess night is one of his most favorite activities. For fun, he started an investment club and shares profits and lessons with his investors on the stock exchange.

Over a few months, Garth clearly had undergone a significant transformation and radiated a picture of robust health. Retirement clearly was good for him. Best of all is that Garth has shed more than 20 pounds, and his blood pressure has never been better, according to his wife.

Garth's progress along the PERMA-V model was impressive. He started by chasing his passion and found meaning which led to engagement. He formed relationships around the activities that in turn supported his vitality and fomented a positive outlook, a happy disposition, and general satisfaction with his life.

Taking Stock

After all is said and done, what can we say about the mechanics of planning for retirement? The four examples may offer different insights, but there's no escaping the one undisputed truth—know yourself to know where you are heading.

Planning, or at least effective planning, merely adds the route markers and milestones to your map.

Some thoughts may help show the way:

- Positivity: Are you planning to retire with a happy and healthy outlook?

- Engagement: Are you willing to make each moment count?

- Do you have a wish-list of things to do?

- Do you understand the difference between a plan and going with the flow and hoping to hit the happiness jackpot?

  - If that's the case, is it a deliberate choice to live life as it comes?

    - Some seniors revel in this approach, often as the first, or the freedom, stage in their retirement.

- See it for what it is, be clear in your mind that it's a transitional stage.

- Distinguish between relaxing and mindlessly drifting, as in drinking beer in front of the TV all day.

- Avoid the creeping phenomenon of shrinkage in all aspects of your life.

  ○ Meaning: Keep your mind active.

  ○ Vitality: Exercise your body and its muscles.

  ○ Relationships: Maintain social interactions with friends, ex-colleagues, and neighbors.

  ○ Achievement: Cultivate other interests such as the arts, theater, knitting, or gardening.

About Plans…

All successful plans default to flexibility setting. A change of any sort doesn't mean the plan has failed, but it needs to adapt to whatever circumstances or conditions have cropped up.

Early-stage planning is about charting a general course ahead, not latching onto route markers because that's what the plan says.

- Think of a checklist of things to do, people to connect with, and places to see.

- Sketch broad outcomes, goals, and desires.

- Take the steps you can toward those ambitions.

  ○ Act with purpose. Be deliberate in your actions.

Looking forward to something special is one of life's real pleasures. Putting these desires to paper is the best possible start to making the dream come true.

Balancing to Flourish

Life after work, just like life during work, is a balancing act of priorities to improve your quality of life. It's an ongoing, evolving part of our lives that American psychologist Dr Martin Seligman has framed into a desire to 'flourish.' As explained in the introduction of this book, Seligman's PERMA-V model is based on positive emotions, engagement, relationships, meaning, accomplishments, and vitality.

As we saw in the case studies earlier, to 'flourish' means to live with purpose and meaning. This quality varies enormously from person to person but clearly plays a role in how your future unfolds.

Stations on the Journey

A common theme among retired people is the bump-and-start syndrome. That's when people undergo various emotions in response to events they didn't

34

anticipate. Hank and Lyn are classic examples. You can roughly break it down to the following stages:

- Holiday time. Life's a party, let's go!

- Bewilderment. Partying loses its fizz, boredom sets in.

  - Disillusion and depression follow.

- Insight. Onus is on you to salvage your retirement

  - Take initiative.

- Solution. You find your groove.

  - happy mix of mental, physical challenges

  - positive relationships

  - warm and friendly socialization.

Under the Hat

We recently sat down with Jock on the terrace—where else—after a particularly dramatic sunset. We couldn't think of a better view or a more beautiful place where we'd rather spend our third trimester on Earth.

Not everybody is as privileged as we are, and it started us thinking about what it takes to make retirement as worthwhile as possible,

We came up with the following suggestions that probed some awkward, but important, things to think about as you consider your tailored retirement.

- Timing. When do I want to stop working?

- Do I want to relocate or downsize?

- Where?

- Why there?

- Top 3 must-do things list

- Who will I be with?

  o What do they want to do?

  o What happens when they pass on?

- Where do I meet other like-minded people?

- How do I stay healthy and mobile to enjoy my new life?

  o What do I need to start, stop, or do more of?

- How do I give back to my community?

  o What skills, expertise, or passion can I share?

Chapter 3:

Next Level Decision-Making

Do you wonder why some people are better at making decisions than others? We're talking about committing to a course of action, not whether a decision is necessarily good or bad. Some people are decisive, others are dithering.

As we'll see, there is value in thinking long and hard before making a decision. In fact, careful consideration is critical for making a decision that affects your life. It's equally true that delaying a decision may also affect your life and not for the best.

Decisions, Decisions...

This topic came up when we discussed the plight of Joe, the town's long-serving lighthouse keeper. It was a lonely job with a peculiar routine—manning the lighthouse tower from 6 p.m. to 6 a.m.—and catching up on sleep during the day.

He lived in the lightkeeper's cottage, about 200 yards from the lighthouse, and became somewhat of a recluse after his wife died 15 years ago. He was liked, and people were fond of him in a distant sort of way.

His illness caught everybody by surprise. The cashier at the grocer was shocked at his appearance and raised the alarm with the town council, his employer. It turned out that Joe had been diagnosed with rheumatoid arthritis (RA) more than a year ago but kept the news to himself,

The auto-immune disease clearly was taking its toll, and Joe found it increasingly difficult to manage the 186 steps to the top of the lighthouse. Keeping the hours also became difficult, but not once did Joe complain or even mention the difficulty.

When asked why he didn't share the diagnosis, Joe said he had nobody to tell. Besides, what difference would that have made to his condition, he asked.

Everything about Joe and his actions, or rather lack of action, was against what PERMA-V advocated. Joe lacked the positivity and optimism, he had no relationships to speak of, there was very little meaning beyond his lighthouse duties, and he experienced very little vitality.

Joe's response to his plights struck us as being incredibly sad. A loyal, conscientious man in a small, tight-knit community who suffered the pain of his degenerative illness alone.

The conundrum was also hugely disempowering for Joe. The cold and damp conditions of the lighthouse made his RA worse. He was strongly advised to change his environment, adopt a strict diet, and take his medication.

Decision Default

Joe defaulted on all three recommendations. He didn't renew his prescription after it had run out after three months, his recluse life made a restrictive diet impossible, and he made no plans to get out of the lighthouse.

Joe rationalized his behavior in the oddest way. He said things weren't so bad because he still managed to do the job. He also poo-pooed suggestions that preemptive action could have made his life a lot better.

In Joe's case, the fear of change skewed his decision making. His reluctance to make decisive decisions outweighed the possible benefits of interventions. In the end, Joe had no control over the decisions that determined his future.

The local church's outreach committee adopted Joe's plight and arranged for a high-care nurse to visit him at home. A decent pension meant that Joe would get the care he needed.

Not all decision-making is hesitant, of course. Some people are impressively decisive about their decisions, as in the case of a fiercely independent and feisty 70-year-old woman.

Fearless and Feisty

Our town has its fair share of unique characters with feisty Freda a prime example. She and her husband moved here many moons ago to open the town's first bakery. They worked hard, and their selection of breads, buns, and patisserie found favor with town folk.

While tending to the bread oven one morning, Freda's husband dropped dead after suffering a massive heart attack. Freda was devastated, but the support from the community convinced her to continue with the bakery.

The long hours took their toll on her health. A hip replacement operation persuaded her to sell the business and downsize to a unit in the retirement complex.

The sedentary lifestyle, limited mobility, and a love for cake and cream saw Freda put on an alarming 45 lbs (20 kg) over a few months. Less than a year after retiring, Freda started to show symptoms of type 2 diabetes. The extra weight also put pressure on her knees, and she found it increasingly difficult to take Tiki, her Maltese poodle, for a walk.

The pre-diabetes diagnosis was Freda's wake-up call. At the age of 70, she changed her diet and joined the aerobics exercise class at the retirement complex. Disciplined and determined, she shed more than 35 lbs (15 kg) and was able to walk Tiki every day. Even better, she was able to stop her pre-diabetes medication.

If her transformation was a surprise, she blew people away with her next move—selling her retirement unit and hitting the road in a motorhome with Tiki.

We were gobsmacked. We had so many questions, but only one really mattered: What about the future?

She smiled. "All my life, I lived for the future. Now I want to live in the future," she said. "For me, the journey is the destination."

Freda had also hooked up with a network of like-minded adventurers who organize get-togethers and host fellow members on their travels. With the help of the internet, she found like-minded souls in other parts of the world too, including RVingWomen, Sole Travelers, even Rolling Solos and Wander Women.

What happens when the RV jaunt runs out of road?

"Well," she said, "when I'm done with traveling, or I can't anymore, I'll move into a high-care unit. Don't worry, it's paid for already."

There was nothing more to say. Freda wasn't acting on impulse. She knew exactly what she had wanted. Freda's planning and determination made it possible to travel independently.

Freda gave an entirely new meaning to the PERMA-V philosophy. She positively basked in engagement and actively sought out new relationships in a passionate drive, quite literally, for meaning. Little wonder that she demonstrated more vitality than many younger and healthier people.

Different Strokes

Henry and I went back a long time. We first met as young students attending the same physical training academy before going our separate ways. We kept in touch over the years and met up from time to time at seminars and conferences hosted by our industry organization.

Our last conversation stayed in my mind for a long time because it challenged some of the common ideas about retirement. Henry proved that "playing for time" and not making a firm decision does have its merits under certain conditions.

Henry's circumstances were unusual. While he was in a position to retire earlier, his wife, 10 years younger than him, was not. She was at the height of her career, and cashing in her chips early made no sense.

Henry was looking forward to more free time but also worried about having too much time on his hands.

He had several interests—golf, sports, and travel—but he wasn't particularly passionate about any of them.

He certainly had no interest in most outdoor pursuits like gardening, fishing, or hiking. Nor did he have a particularly large circle of friends.

After much navel-gazing and discussions with his wife, he chose a middle path—part-time employment. This route allowed him to

- maintain his professional interest

- scale down the hours at work

- pursue his current interests

- keep an eye out for new opportunities

- develop a retirement plan.

This path suits him and his wife down to a tee. What else matters but ensuring flexibility.

Barriers, Real and Imagined

People make decisions for different reasons. Not making a decision is also a decision, of course. There's a difference between not making a decision and delaying a decision, though. It is important to understand the difference as the three cases hopefully illustrate.

What about perceived obstacles that hold us back from making a decision? Close to home, I think of my wife who learned to ride a bicycle when she was 42. Unbelievable, right?

All her life, Colette feared falling off more than she was scared about getting on a bike. As a child, she wouldn't let her father take off the training wheels and never learned to ride.

The switch came when Colette—an unashamed Francophile—was offered a wine, dine, and cycle holiday to France. The lure was too much to resist, and she finally confronted her fear.

With some coaxing and a helping hand, Colette finally let go of her fears. To her delight, riding a bicycle proved a lot easier than she had feared. The prospect of a leisurely sojourn through Provence astride a bicycle was enough to break down the resistance.

The same paralyzing fear also holds us back from other options in life. Keith, an old schoolmate, used every excuse in the book, and then some, to avoid thinking about retirement.

Keith would shake his head and say "finances hold the key to retirement" before launching into a long explanation about the rising costs of food, housing, health, medical care, transport, and the ills of inflation. There's no point talking about retirement if he could not afford it, Keith said.

It was a clever but short-sighted ruse. Keith's financial worries drew a curtain over any discussion about retirement. More than that, it also pushed the impending reality of retirement into the distance.

The tactic backfired badly when Keith fell off a ladder and fractured his pelvis. Unable to work and facing hefty medical bills, Keith was forced into retirement long before he was ready. Imagine, if he had done the planning even though he wasn't ready to act he would have been much better prepared to deal with his circumstances.

Rubber Meeting the Road

If you're waiting for the right time or a sudden passion to strike as a sign for you to retire, you may be waiting a long time.

Instead, focus on what you know and the real issues to be addressed. They typically include

- questions and concerns about income

- worries about staying busy and not falling into lethargy

- realistic appraisals about

    o where you are at

    o what you want

    o how to achieve your goals.

Break from the Past

Sometimes stubbornly clinging to what we know may actually hold us back. You may even hang onto past achievements, awards, or rewards as justifications for not changing. It's a lot like saying that something doesn't need fixing if it's not broken, except it is broken. It's really a kind of delaying tactic that is to be avoided.

Best to accept the past, move on, and think about the future. In our experience, to do that, you need to embrace the present and live each day to its fullest.

Live in the Present

It's amazing what difference a few positive habits can make to the quality of each day. These routines can take different forms and very much depend on the individual. It makes sense to start the morning with a routine that sets the tone for the day. It may be a yoga session, a stretch routine, meditation, deep breathing, or smelling the roses. Find your happy habit. One that puts you in a positive frame of mind for what's to come.

Cultivate a reflective day-end ritual. It could be a mindful stroll around the garden, a meditative moment of gratitude, some journalling or time of silence and contemplation.

Create your habits to live intentionally in the present and eagerly anticipate your future.

Are You Ready?

Have you figured out whether your concerns are real, imagined, or things you haven't worked through yet? If you're still unsure, try this:

- List the three things that make you most nervous.

- Next to each concern, write what you would do if it was NOT an issue.

- Write down what you can do to either fix or reduce the anxiety.

- Rank the actions from easy to hard.

- Tackle one easy and one tough step per week.

- Start with easy, small steps, one per week.

- See how you feel after six to eight weeks.

Some of these suggestions may seem somewhat pedantic, but they're really aimed at asking the tough questions and finding answers. Confront the process, make it your own. Create the future you want and deserve.

Chapter 4:

Purpose—What's The Point?

The transition from a working life to retirement can be tough. For some retirees, the reality of retirement is a far cry from their expectations and often leads to disillusionment and deep unhappiness.

It's a surprisingly common occurrence that, according to an American study, sees about 40% of retirees reversing their decision to retire (Maestas, 2010).

It's a perplexing phenomenon that shines a torch on both the preparedness for your third age and the shock of unexpected emotions experienced by some new retirees.

Quite how disenchanted retirees deal with their contrarian feelings very much depends on the individual. But there's little doubt that a sense of purpose—or lack of it—plays a key role in their appreciation of retirement.

The experience of Sally and Karl below illustrates the point.

Sally: All's Not Well in Paradise

Richard and Sally Cornhill were popular dinner guests who regularly graced our table. They were both retired professionals—he a lawyer and she an accountant—and were knowledgeable about an impressive range of topics with a shared passion for red wine.

Also joining us for dinner one sublime evening on the terrace over a few bottles of a superb Malbec vintage were Mick and Mary, friends from our previous lives as business consultants.

They met Richard and Sally for the first time that evening and clearly were taken by the poster couple for retirement. Urbane, affluent, and engaging, the Cornhills radiated success and contentment. But appearance can be deceiving, as we discovered.

Raising her glass, Mary looked around the table: "So, what do lucky people like you think of retirement in this beautiful place? How's your life of leisure panning out for you all?"

Sally rose unsteadily and almost knocked over her glass.

"I'll tell you. It's one way traffic, all the way. From here 'til kingdom comes. It sucks."

Richard tried to soothe her, but she brushed him off.

"No, I haven't had too much to drink. And yes, I'm speaking the truth, believe you me."

My wife rescued the awkwardness. Ever the gracious hostess, Colette led Sally to the kitchen to help her serve coffee.

Richard laughed off Sally's outburst and blamed it on a glass or two too many of the exceptional vintage. But something clearly was badly out of kilter.

Karl: Crash Landing

Few retirees were more disenchanted with their golden age than Karl. Freshly retired after a high-flying career as a pilot and sought-after private aircraft broker, Karl fell into a deep unhappiness. None of the trappings of luxury—a stunning unit with forever views, deep pockets, and a vintage Porsche in the garage—softened the discontent.

It did not take long to figure out that the problem wasn't boredom but a lack of meaningful purpose. The doors of perception creaked open and signaled the start of Karl's much more rewarding second journey.

His journey of redemption made for an inspiring flight path, one that closely tracked the universal theme of thirsting after the meaning and purpose of life.

Taking Stock

Sally and Karl might have been on different life trajectories, but they suffered the same disappointment about their twilight years.

Sally reluctantly followed her husband's lead who had wanted her to retire so that they could spend more time traveling in the motorhome they had bought. That was all fine and well, except they also spent a lot of time at home.

The problem was that while Richard was having a whale of time playing golf and racket-ball and riding with his mates, Sally was at a loss and felt abandoned. Moping around their home, albeit a beautiful one, was not her idea of a fulfilling retirement.

Over time, her annoyance morphed into resentment at being left to fend for herself.

Karl, on the other hand, experienced a deep-seated loss of self-worth. The shift from being a serious player in the aviation industry to being relegated to the sidelines affected him deeply, something he did not anticipate.

Both Sally and Karl were at a cross-roads. In their separate ways, they sensed they were short-changing themselves. The question was how to address their respective shortcomings.

Retirement Redemption

Sally and Karl were in agreement on a fundamental principle: They did not want to rewind the clock to life before retirement. Too much time had elapsed, and they both wanted more from what was left of their lives. In other words, they wanted to find meaning in their respective new lives and not default to their previous lives.

It's an important realization in the greater scheme of things. Finding purpose and meaning is a key tenet in the quest for happiness, or in Dr Martin Seligman's words, "to flourish."

Sally and Karl followed different routes to achieving contentment in their retirement.

Sally: Beating Her Own Path

To Sally's credit, she took her time to think about what was troubling her. Besides, rushing the process might not have yielded the solution she had wanted.

Over many hours of reflection, Sally realized she owed it to herself to share what she had wanted. She also had to acknowledge that it's not always possible or practical to do everything together. It was time for a rethink on how they make decisions.

Consensus is not always possible, and compromises also fall short as neither party achieves true happiness. Besides, during their working lives, they often derived pleasure from different activities; why should it be different in retirement?

Sally wasn't particularly concerned about achieving a greater purpose in retirement. Instead, she wanted to fill the spaces between traveling and touring with rewarding activities.

She experimented and explored several interests. At first, it was a hit-and-miss scenario, but soon she settled into a routine that involved bushwalking and hiking, fitness classes, regular volunteer work, joining a gardening club, and making time to care for their grandchildren.

In time, Sally settled into a fulfilling and rewarding retirement rhythm. It became a comforting and comfortable routine that she was more than happy to discuss and share with other people.

Karl: Recalibrating Reality

Karl faced up to some unsettling truths about himself. He came to realize that he needed validation of who he was. Karl also acknowledged that he wanted to be valued for his contribution to society.

He needed to find purpose and meaning in retirement. The first thing he did was to get a grip on his anxiety. It was time to think long and hard about what he had left behind in order to discover what he had wanted for his retirement.

Drawing on his innate sense of order and logic, Karl took uncompromising stock of his skills and abilities. He paid particular attention to a natural inclination for structure and his focus on attention to detail. He also ticked off his natural affinity for people and his considerable trove of interpersonal skills—qualities that had propelled him to the great heights he had achieved in his working life.

In particular, he acknowledged a passion for seeing people succeed. It was a characteristic he had developed over many years as a pilot behind the controls of different aircraft and sharpened as a respected team leader.

Gradually, his natural pragmatism came to the fore. In his mind, Karl calibrated his compass in the knowledge that if his chosen direction did not lead him to his planned destination, he would explore other options.

Karl narrowed down his options to a shortlist. First, he joined the local Vintage Car Club. After a short while, he deployed his management skills to help with administration at the club. The involvement paved the way for taking greater responsibility and helping to guide the club toward a sounder footing for the benefit of members and guests.

The same passion for iconic cars he applied to another long-neglected pastime: playing golf. His previous life did not allow for a more satisfying handicap, a shortcoming he addressed with great enthusiasm. Apart from knocking down his handicap, Karl also got some valuable time in the open and made new friends walking the course.

Finally, Karl made an approach to the local flight school. It was a call that turbo-charged the purpose in his life. His enviable knowledge and deep insight struck a ringing chord with the academy, its instructor, and students. Soon, he started to volunteer his experience and expertise and found himself as a popular mentor of young pilots

Karl discovered that by giving more of himself, he satisfied a deep urge to make a meaningful difference to the lives of other people. It was a revelatory insight that changed his life, for the better.

Meaningful Purpose

The desire to give back is a powerful force not always properly understood. It's more than just an altruistic response to help others not as privileged as you are. Often, it is motivated by a sense of a deeper or greater purpose.

The sentiment takes different forms, most commonly through volunteer work. Think of people with experience and expertise offering their time to coach or mentor others with the express purpose of making a difference, be it professionally or personally.

To be clear, we're not talking about charity or freebie hand-outs but a commitment to help others in whatever endeavor they're aspiring to.

For some, being a loving partner, parent, or grandparent is reason enough to reach out and be the best role model they can be.

Other people with a deeply-entrenched sense of community go the extra mile by sharing themselves unreservedly with no expectation of reward or recompense. It's a priceless gift.

Little wonder that the beneficiaries of this kind of selflessness recall these acts of kindness with deep gratitude and appreciation in their personal journeys of growth and development.

Lessons of Note

Finding purpose in life means different things to people. The quest assumes an even greater urgency once you enter the third age of your life.

It's a life-positive mission that the longest-serving first lady of the U.S., the charismatic Eleanor Roosevelt, understood only too well.

"The purpose of life is to live it, to taste experience to the utmost, to reach out eagerly without fear for newer & richer experience" (Branch, 2015).

For some, it is about fulfilling a passion; for others, it is unearthing a passion they did not know that they had.

No matter how you spin it, the search demands of you to step out of your comfort zone. It's not always an easy thing to do, but drawing on your past experiences may just give you the courage and strength you need.

One of the most transformative actions is the power of volunteering, or giving of yourself. It's a sentiment perfectly summed up in a quote despite being falsely attributed to British statesman Winston Churchill: "We make a living by what we get. We make a life by what we give" (Quotes Falsely Attributed to Winston Churchill, 2008).

Some pointers worth pondering:

- What do you want out of retirement?
  - Does it mean pursuing more than one objective?
    - Joining a walking group?
    - Meeting people?
    - Become healthier?
    - Exploring new places?
- What about giving back to society?
  - Have you considered volunteering?
    - Does it align with your values and principles?
    - Does it bring you joy and pleasure?
- Do you have some ideas, goals, or activities to share?
- Can you list three things to try or practice?

Chapter 5:

Growth—Don't Shut Up Shop, Put In and Enjoy the Growth Factor

Few sights are more disconcerting than a group of residents in a high-care facility who have given up on life. Their demeanor says it all. Miserable and morose, they're confined to a bed or a wheelchair as they stare sunken-eyed at the end of their lives.

For them, life has lost meaning in a defeatist resignation of what is left of their time on earth. The sad reality started long before their physical isolation and can be traced to their mental surrender many years ago.

It's a state of mind that is entirely preventable. Entering the third phase of your life doesn't mean shutting out the world and calling quits on your happiness. On the contrary, as retirees who thrive with a zest of life will tell you, retirement is not the end but the beginning of a new appreciation of the wonders of life.

Fixed Mindset vs Growth Mindset

The difference between people who thrive and those who survive is a mental approach. Or, as psychologist Elizabeth Dweck says, your mindset shapes your motivation. Prof. Dweck is an authority on the subject and has spent the better part of her professional life refining the concepts she pioneered—a fixed mindset against a growth mindset. (Cote, 2022)

The difference can be illustrated with any number of simple examples. Think of two wannabe entrepreneurs—one with a fixed mindset who fears that lack of financial acumen stops them from pursuing a business career, and the other with a growth mindset who believes that the skills can be learned and is excited about the opportunity. Any guesses which of the two individuals is set for a path of success?

The same scenario can be applied to a retirement context. Imagine two retirees—one who is content to ride out retirement with what they have, and another who goes out on a limb to make the most of their third age.

As a good friend who loves to come up with clever quips once said, "Retirement is not a spectator sport."

Shane: Life is for Living

Speaking of a sporting analogy, I once was introduced to a remarkable fellow with a passion for life second to none. Shane proved in no uncertain fashion that life is for living and that age is not a barrier to, well, anything.

Shane was also a serial entrepreneur with a frightening intellect who saw opportunity where most of us saw hard work and high risk. Having founded three fintech endeavors that trawled the mysterious world of cryptocurrencies, Shane cashed out the world of finance for a life of greater leisure.

Even before retiring early at the age of 58, Shane was an active mountain biker who had put us, his cycling buddies, to shame with his fitness and focus. His sights were set on conquering a new sport, that of kiteboarding, or as it is known elsewhere in the world, kitesurfing.

He took to the thrills of skimming the water like a dolphin surfing the waves. With his trademark single-minded focus, Shane soon mastered the intricacies of riding the wind and held his own against kiteboarders half his age.

Shane became a highly proficient kiteboarder, and his quest for greater technical expertise took him to Mexico for six months of the year.

His Mexican sojourn was more than just an excuse to indulge in the warm waters of his favorite destination, the Yucatan Peninsula. It also allowed him plenty of opportunity to meet and engage with locals and foreigners drawn to the exotic attractions of Mexico.

Kiteboarding, as Shane explained, was the ultimate deal breaker. More than exposure to one of the most exhilarating physical experiences imaginable, it also challenged his mental prowess and emotional resilience.

Sure, kiteboarding can be dangerous and is physically demanding. But there's no doubt that harnessing the wind has also unleashed the power of his mind. The physical and mental focus necessary to kiteboard helps to clear his mind and open it to new opportunities. Skimming over the water's surface gives vent to his passion, one of the interests on his short list now. As the saying goes, the sky's the limit.

Shane chose to continue finding challenges like kiteboarding rather than accept a more static approach. His quest for change and growth continues to drive him.

June: Sculpting Happiness

June was a much-loved stalwart at the local hospital. A maternity ward sister who had helped more babies into the world than she had cared to remember, June started to count down the months to retirement.

It was a time filled with reflection and contemplation. Soon, her life would no longer be filled by the demands that had defined her daily existence for almost 30 years.

As a nursing professional, mother, and wife, June's life was consumed by caring for other people. Over time, she had neglected her own needs and pleasures, a vacuum that reminded her of times long gone.

June recalled the days as a young nurse at a clinic in a small farming community. For fun, she scraped off the clay from the cattle grid left by the hooves of cattle and molded animal faces and heads, much to the delight of her young children.

Inspired by the simple pleasures of clay sculpting, June enrolled for classes at a local pottery studio. She reduced the number of hours at the hospital and used the extra time to learn new sculpting skills.

Bonus was meeting other potters of all ability as she honed her own skills and learned the intricacies of throwing and firing her own pots. Before formally retiring, June discovered a talent for Raku pottery. Her creations won favor with family and friends and in time generated a lucrative income.

She re-fired her past passion and found new challenges in doing so.

Listen Up: An Active Mind in an Active Body

The experiences of Shane and June are by no means unique. We all know, or are aware of, seniors pushing their limits to test their boundaries. They intuitively sense a need to stimulate their brain and know that keeping their faculties alive and well is critical to their well-being.

Science bears out their hunch, that cerebral atrophy is public enemy number one. That's why addressing hearing loss is a critical staging post in the fight against aging. More than just an inconvenience, hearing loss is the leading modifiable factor—something you can do about—to stave off dementia by an astounding 200% to 500% (Trott, 2018).

The reason is that untreated hearing loss affects the key brain functions of memory, language, and speech. Being hard of hearing means that parts of a conversation can go missing, which leaves you in an uncomfortable spot. Odds are you will opt out of a conversation and perhaps dodge social engagements because they're too awkward, or even embarrassing, to deal with.

The excuse becomes a familiar refrain: "I can't hear nor participate, and it's frustrating for everyone."

You're not doing yourself, or any other people, any favors by choosing to withdraw from society. All you're doing is shrinking your world that almost certainly will lead to cognitive decline. Choose the path that opens doors, not closes down your world.

Use It or Lose It

Much as sound hearing is a critical bellwether of brain health, other functions are no less important. Think of a competitive bodybuilder who has worked exceptionally hard to build muscle, fitness, and health.

It's by no means a finite process, and maintaining a winning physique demands ongoing training, fastidious nutrition, and a razor-sharp mental focus. Neglect any of these building blocks, and they will sacrifice all the hard work they had put into achieving their ideals.

The same philosophy applies to most mortals who strive for a happy, active, and fulfilled life. Dial back on the hard work and expect a loss of focus and diminished health, physically, mentally, and emotionally.

Tune Into the Zone

We're all familiar with the expression "time flies." It's when you're so engrossed in what you're doing that you literally lose track of time. Finding your mojo is not always easy, and sometimes it's a case of finding an activity that is challenging enough to absorb your focus but not so difficult that you throw in the towel.

The trick is teasing out the reward of a hobby, or learning a new skill, even a language, that occupies your mind 100%. Take comfort in the research that shows, time and again, that your growth is achieved by challenging yourself.

It's always easier finding an activity that engages you. Often it takes discipline and effort, but rest assured, your purpose is out there. It just needs to be found.

In a perfect world, whatever you choose should engage your mind, promote muscle tone, and also encourage movement and flexibility.

Power of the Brain

The brain is by far the most important organ in the human body. Our thoughts dictate every single human desire, impulse, and activity, from solving a complex puzzle to chipping a golf ball onto the green and finding inspiration.

Truth be told, we're faced by a bewildering number of choices to exercise your mind. Think of

- left and right brain challenges that promote different growth

- learning French, Spanish, or any other language

- mastering a musical instrument

- exploring various apps or even paper games, from Sudoku to Wordle

- playing strategic board games like chess, backgammon, or even checkers.

Let's not overlook those activities that engage our mind, body, and even your soul. Some examples include

- dancing that promotes movement, agility, and memory

- acting and singing that stimulates mental activity, memory, and breath control

- cycling that promotes physical activity, balance, and breathing

- pottery and sculpting that expresses a vision and promotes hand-eye coordination.

On Reflection

Humans are by far the most complex species on Earth. Our bodies have evolved to move, our minds are made to be challenged, and our emotions are wired for happiness and stimulation.

We need to take guidance from our human reality. Drawing on a sporting example, a personal trainer in a gym will challenge you to improve and grow by means of the age-old principle of "progressive overload" by forcing your body to push beyond the familiarity of a set routine.

In the same way, the advent of calculators stopped us from engaging our brain to perform simple mental arithmetic calculations.

The onus is on us as human beings to remain engaged and not slide into inactivity once we bid the working world adieu. If anything, the advent of the third age should spur us to explore areas where we hadn't gone before.

Spare a thought for the routines that challenge us physically and mentally. Equally vital are the activities and engagements that stimulate our social life and connect us to our society.

Active Engagement

When all is said and done, it's fair to observe the indisputable truth that retirement is immeasurably better once we've nailed down the mental and physical challenges that enhance the quality of life. The questions worth thinking about are

- Which rewarding activities will challenge you physically?

- Which rewarding activities will challenge you mentally?

- Which rewarding activities will challenge you socially?

- How can you access any of these activities?

- How can you explore any of these activities further?

Go find the activities and people that challenge your norms and help you to keep growing in all areas of a life worth living.

Chapter 6:

Social Interaction—Facebook Doesn't Count... Enough

The Covid pandemic has transformed the world in ways we couldn't possibly have foreseen. One of the biggest changes was the way humans forced into isolation had to adapt to a new way of communicating. Almost overnight, we had to learn how to connect remotely through virtual meetings, online conversations, and Zoom sessions.

Digital technology may have helped us to stay in touch, but it also exposed the severe limitations of faceless contact. It didn't take humans in quarantine long to realize that there was no substitute for the real thing, that personal contact is a human condition for happiness.

Psychologists are acutely aware of the risks associated with a lack of social interaction. They know that people deprived of human contact are prone to developing anxiety, depression, heart disease, and quite possibly, a diminished quality of life.

Humans are wired for social connections. Research tells us that we need to form and maintain strong, stable interpersonal relationships. Not only do rewarding relationships make people happy, they also influence our health and promote a longer, more fulfilling life (Oppong, 2019).

A Lament of Loss

People approaching retirement are especially vulnerable to social isolation. It's a condition that creeps up on you, often without you realizing it.

No matter how you spin it, retirement implies a degree of dislocation and loss. Yes, it may mean a physical relocation in one way or another, but it also means giving up on some of our connections and relationships. Severing your work-based networks is an obvious example. So too is packing up your life and moving away to another part of the country, or even a different part of the world.

Staying Alive, Keeping in Touch

The only answer to the dreaded sense of loss is not losing out on what you have. It's easier said than done, but two complementary factors apply. Firstly, you have to maintain the connections you have, and secondly, you have to nurture new relationships wherever you find yourself.

Neither of these routes are necessarily easy options. Both courses of action demand attention and commitment. But ask yourself if you have a choice. For the sake of the happiness of you and your significant other, you need social interactions. How you achieve those is the million Dollar question.

James and Karen: Build, Operate, and Maintain

I met James, a senior engineer with a large multinational civil construction company who had retired to our neck of the woods. A jovial golfer with an infectious laugh and a wicked drive, James was looking forward to bringing down his handicap.

His other passions were woodworking and a love for the church of which he and Karen, his wife, had been active members of many years.

Their decision to join our community made perfect sense, explained James. The links course was right up his alley, the local woodworkers guild was active, and their church had welcomed its newest congregants with open arms.

They realized that the move from the city would be a wrench. The children and grandchildren were a good few hours away, and they would have to forge a new life. On the plus side, they had put their faith in their well-rounded sense of community.

They were not disappointed. Karen's business acumen blew a breath of fresh air into the church's three charity shops, while James was sharpening his lathe and putting skills with equal vigor.

Next, they were invited to the tennis club and joined the walking group on its weekly ramblings along the coast and through the countryside. They pursued these activities with enthusiasm and joined networks across different activities.

Separately and together, James and Karen found purpose and pleasure in their new lives.

Yes, they missed their family and old friends, but new-fangled Zoom and other digital platforms kept up the regular contact. Planning for face-to-face meetups on special occasions, like Christmas, Easter, and birthdays, was real fun, said James.

"It's not about substituting one life for another," he said, "it's about adding a fresh dimension to what you have already."

James and Karen dealt with the conundrum before it could become a problem. Their solution was a sensible compromise—actively maintain contact with longstanding friends and family, and vigorously seek out and build new relationships and friendships through activities they either enjoyed or were willing to explore.

Their chosen path has ticked several boxes; they've expanded their social network, stimulated growth by learning new skills and improving others, and started being active outdoors. Together, James and Karen rang all the bells for a life that flourishes.

Aunt Laura: Purpose in Renewal

Aunt Laura, an 80-something widow, had experienced her fair share of life's ups and downs. Both her sons had died from cancer, and she had outlived many of her friends. Still in reasonably good health, Aunt Laura nevertheless found herself increasingly isolated.

Through no fault of her own, she was spending more time alone and saw less of her family and friends.

Her world was growing smaller by the day. Leaving her apartment became more difficult, and she no longer visited the two galleries or attended the ballet. The soirees she so enjoyed also fell by the wayside.

Her seclusion started to feed on itself. Aunt Laura not only started to suffer memory lapses but also retreated into the past. When she was nor repeating the same story for the umpteenth time, she was forgetting what she was saying. Outings simply did not appeal. Visiting Aunt Laura was becoming very awkward and near impossible to enjoy.

Finally, during a routine health checkup, she was diagnosed with a mild form of dementia.

A niece with time on her hands stepped in. She wouldn't take 'no' for an answer, loaded Aunt Laura in her car, and took her galivanting.

They took in the galleries, went to foreign film showings, and had lunch at her favorite bistro.

Over the next two years, Aunt Laura socialized and stimulated her mind more than she did the previous 10 years.

It was a massive turn-around with an incredible outcome. Gradually, her confidence increased and memory improved. From being the reclusive mouse hiding away in her apartment, Aunt Laura had blossomed into a gracious lady with a love for modern art and a fondness for cerebral conversation over coffee and cake. The person we remembered fondly.

What Just Happened?

So what really happened here? A little late but never too late, Aunt Laura's niece intervened. Her never-say-die mission forced Aunt Laura to re-engage with the outside world and revel in the activities she loved.

Apart from building up Aunt Laura's confidence, the intervention also paved the way for meeting like-minded people. Aunt Laura expanded her social networks and reconnected her life with family and new friends.

The upshot is that Aunt Laura is feeling far more positive about life. The vitality buried in her seclusion has returned with a vengeance. Aunt Laura is back!

Unlike Aunt Laura, don't wait for someone else to intervene. It's up to you to stay socially and mentally engaged. And it's much more fun than staying at home. The sooner the better.

Social Isolation and Loneliness

Several studies show that social isolation and the lack of contact from family and friends is bad for your health (Ortiz-Ospina and Roser, 2020).

What if you're not a social butterfly that wings it on other people's energy and presence? What if you're an introvert who, truth be told, actually prefers your own company?

The good news is that there is no one-size-fits-all solution. Everybody is unique and inspired by different things. Perhaps you need no more than an hour or two a week of chin wagging with your friends, while your neighbors may thrive on double or even triple that amount of time.

The trick is to find what works for you. It's for the good of your mental health, so be mindful about your choices.

Choices, Choices

Sometimes the most rewarding engagements happen when you least expect it. Moving into a retirement complex, for example, may be daunting at first. You may not know anybody or feel at a loss because your family and friends are not in close distance.

Under those circumstances, it's easy to forget that other people are often in the same boat. You may all suffer the same disconnection, reason enough to reach out and find common ground. You are, after all, all living in the same community, share the same space, and even plug into the same networks.

The best advice is reaching out to like-minded others. Once you've connected with them, learn to grow with them. Often the most difficult step is the first one. Once you've broken the ice, it becomes a lot easier to move forward together. You may surprise yourself at how rewarding the process of moving forward becomes, even if you stumble the first few times. The very act of reaching out and meeting others is self-propelling, making it easier next time. What's stopping you?

Points to Ponder

There's no doubt that social interaction is vital for your happiness and fulfillment. Physical connections are at the center of our human existence, and it's up to you to make sure those relationships are healthy and vibrant.

It takes effort, sometimes extraordinary effort, to build, maintain, and operate those connections. The pressure mounts when you retire and possibly relocate elsewhere.

Reflecting on our unique situation and after numerous conversations with people facing a similar scenario, a few pointers stand out. See if any resonate with you on your journey to staying connected.

Treasure Your Relationships

Protect what you have with every ounce of your ability. Go beyond the extra mile to safeguard the personal contact with family and friends. Use modern technology to maintain contact. It's far better than no contact. Make a special effort to celebrate important events and occasions. Experience the joy with others.

Accept the Inevitable

The march of time robs us of our nearest and dearest. If it's not illness and death interfering, then distance and time also take away the closeness. We age, and often family and friends pass on.

That doesn't mean we have to march up to the line and passively wait our turn. We must turn to others and look at ways to build authentic and meaningful connections.

Build New Friendships

Take pleasure in building new networks and friendships. You are not alone in finding a new purpose in life. Seek out like-minded others. Embrace old passions and develop new interests.

Keep the Fires Burning

You are as old, or young, as you choose to be. Make the most of your life. Be curious, be active. Stay engaged. You are an important part of the community. Don't ever forget that.

You have as much to offer the community as the community has to offer you. Be an active part of your community and reap the benefits to you and others. Engaged individuals are what make a flourishing community. Don't forget your role in making that happen.

Chapter 7:

An Attitude of Gratitude

Some of the most inspirational quotes celebrating the human condition pay tribute to gratitude. Perhaps it's the inherent grace of this quality that has moved countless writers, philosophers, and theologians to express their appreciation, respect, and thankfulness for the good things in life.

Swiss theologian Karl Barth had this to say: "Joy is the simplest form of gratitude." Much-loved self-help author Melody Beattie has a more expansive view. "Gratitude unlocks the fullness of life. It turns what we have into enough, and more. It turns denial into acceptance, chaos to order, confusion to clarity. It can turn a meal into a feast, a house into a home, a stranger into a friend" (Shutterfly, 2017).

Stages of Gratitude

There's little doubt about the transformative power of gratitude. Generations of people across the world bear testimony to the power of this quality, not only in its meaning but also in understanding the three stages of gratitude:

- feeling thankful for the positive things in your life

- giving thanks to the people who have made your life happier

- adopting new behaviors as a result of interacting with those who have helped you (Colvin, 2015).

Several studies praise the positive impact of gratitude in people's lives. People who keep journals to "count their blessings" are happier, as our friend Dr. Martin Seligman found. Participants who wrote down three good things each day reported more happiness and less depression after only one month (Seligman et al, 2005).

Motivational speaker Tony Robbins takes thankfulness a step further with his "attitude of gratitude." According to the rags-to-riches billionaire, being grateful for the blessings in your life feeds the law of attraction that in turn delivers more in abundance. Gratitude, it seems, is the bedrock of happiness.

It's a notion deeply entrenched in some cultures that may surprise some Westerners.

So where do you sit on the gratitude and happiness scale? Are you more attuned to what you don't have than what you have? Are your friends generally positive people, or are they a bit negative about the world and our place in it?

Falling into a pattern and habits of negativity is an easy trap... particularly in the times we're living. Let's explore further.

An Epiphany in Spain

I have a very fond memory of a trip through the central western Spanish countryside of Extremadura. We'd been driving for hours, and the sun started to set as we approached a small village with its medieval castle as the unmistakable center of attraction.

It was a hot, blustery afternoon with dust devils dancing through the largely deserted village. But the ancient stone buildings and cobbled streets appealed, and there was something mysteriously alluring about the charming town.

We booked into a small hotel—*un pequeño hotel*—just off the central square. After a refreshing shower and a quick nap, we headed out to explore the incredible architecture dating back to its Roman origins.

A group of elderly men playing cards over small cups of pungent coffee drew our attention. A winning hand was celebrated with friendly banter, and another round was dealt.

As dusk settled, the town slowly came alive. People started coming onto the streets, and waiters hurriedly brought out chairs and tables from inside the bistro.

We noticed the grandmothers, gracious ladies of elderly age, coming together. They strolled together, arms linked, and stopped to have a lively chat with other ladies.

The delight and animation on their faces was a joy to behold. Time with their friends was precious and worth every minute of gossip and laughter.

We witnessed the same joy in children playing hop, skip, and jump with their friends, squealing with delight.

The parents were on the sidelines, watching and chatting with other adults. It was a community alive with happiness and contentment, of pleasure and gratitude. The simple pleasures of the positive and at times playful interactions with close friends or family was evident on their faces and in their gestures. The importance of quality time was clearly understood and appreciated by old and young.

A Very Different Take

The Spanish exposure was very different to anything we had experienced in our Anglo-Saxon culture. Nowhere in our travels in the US, Canada, United Kingdom, or Australia have we seen anything close to what we had witnessed that summer evening in the Extremaduran village.

Back home, people avoid eye-contact and shy away from conversation. In Spain, the townsfolk made the most of the chance to connect. They're also living proof of the human instinct to belong, to be part of a tribe.

The sense of community becomes deeply rewarding when the members of the tribe appreciate each other and revel in the simple pleasures in life. Perhaps not surprisingly, the route to happiness often bypasses the modern tech options and plumb for face-to-face interactions instead. Yet another example of positivity, engagement, and meaningful relationships helping individuals and the community flourish.

Cycles of Life

Barry was an enthusiastic mountain biker who loved nothing more than hitting the trail to escape the drudgery of his suburban routine. All things being equal, Barry was a relatively fit 62-year-old who handled his daily ride with aplomb.

His wife was less enamored with his love for the outdoors astride his Cannondale softail. She worried about some of his longer rides and, on occasion, phoned him to check that he was alright.

Her concern escalated into a full-blown alarm one day when he didn't answer his phone and got back more than an hour late. Hell hath no fury when Barry told her rather sheepishly that he had lost his phone down a steep descent and spent a fruitless hour looking for it.

The penny finally dropped. Barry realized his indulgence was at her expense. He knew that he would not enjoy himself if she was spending her time fretting about his safety.

He scouted around and found a group that met his needs, well almost. The average age of the riders, between 65 and 80, worried him, but not as much as the number of women riders in the group.

How was he going to get the exercise he wanted with a bunch of fuddy-duddies, some of whom were women riders, he grumbled.

But he was committed to at least try out the new experience. As it turned out, Barry was the straggler, and by some distance, on his first ride. To his shock and horror, he could not keep up with the peloton, never mind the pace-setting of the leader of the pack.

Barry was mortified. He was not sure what hurt more— his sore muscles or his bruised ego.

Not that any of the group had made him feel bad for this lack of fitness. In fact, he felt an unexpected warmth toward his new friends over a round of cappuccinos at one of their favorite stops.

That was the beginning of Barry's new life cycle. Against all odds, he found friendship and a renewed vigor to improve his flagging fitness.

As the newest—and youngest—member of the pack, Barry felt compelled to up his game. The positivity and banter blew him away, and he soon became a regular rider who took his turn to set the pace.

Riding with the gray brigade, as the group was known, also opened other doors. One of the regular activities was tending to the garden of the local retirement home, an activity he thoroughly enjoyed.

Pushing the pedal changed his life, Barry joked. Not only had he improved his fitness and shed a few pounds, he also made new friends. He even put a happy smile on the face of his wife.

In his own words, Barry discovered a vitality in the bunch of cyclists that surprised him. Their healthy bodies, and the pleasure of achievement every time they donned lycra, not to mention the laughter and banter in the coffee shop, transcended the age differences.

The love of life and vitality shine a beacon on the possibilities when you "get out there" and be an active part of the world around us.

Life Connections

As humans, we are drawn to the cultural norms that keep us together. We tend to gravitate toward the expectations of safety and comfort that we have in common with other people like us.

Also, strong friendship groups root us to the greater world. So does the love we have for a life partner. However, and powerful as a primary bond is, most of us also need a connection with other members of the human tribe.

Sometimes a loving pet provides the flesh-and-blood connection. There are many reasons for this outreach, but often it's the unconditional love and companionship these sentient beings offer us.

Love, Laughter, and Life

The power of laughter is well documented, from lightening a dark mood to being revered as the ultimate aphrodisiac. Research tells us that laughter unleashes the therapeutic benefits of dopamine and serotonin, the happy drugs our bodies produce naturally (Yim, 2016).

It's no surprise that people with a sunny disposition and a positive mindset are also a lot more content. Living in a state of "conscious appreciation" clearly is good for your mental health and others' happiness.

The opposite end of the spectrum is a lot less fun. Being held captive by despair and depression will affect your state of mind and your happiness. Sadly, we're often victims of society's fixation with so-called news that is really a fixation with sensation.

The constant bombardment of bad news from an armada of media outlets is well-nigh impossible to ignore. It doesn't help that most media are programmed to appeal to the human sense of the catastrophic, a phenomenon known as "negativity bias" (Cherry, 2019).

As psychologist Rick Hanson and other researchers pointed out, the human brain is wired to

- remember bad experiences better than happy ones

- remember insults better than praise

- respond more powerfully to negative impulses

- dwell on negative events more often than positive ones (Cherry, 2019).

More alarmingly, humans tend to believe that bad news is more truthful than good news. We need to ask ourselves why humans choose to believe the worst. Does it somehow make us feel better about our lot? Could it be that we take a weird pleasure from our own unhappiness? Or are we better at dwelling in mindless unhappiness rather than seek mindful happiness?

Whatever the case, we need to identify the negativity cycle in order to break the shackles. You don't want to get caught in the trap of unwittingly freewheeling in the doom-and-gloom until it's too late.

The Good News

Is there any good news in the avalanche of bad news? The answer is a resounding yes because it's up to you to limit or, even better, avoid the barrage of bad news.

Knowledge is power, and it's your choice to help your brain cope better with the unscrupulous efforts by some media to make you a victim of unhappiness.

Surely it's time to stake your rightful claim to happiness and dismiss those fears that hold your mind hostage. In the words of playwright Deborah Bruce, "Stop blaming your fears of tomorrow on your experiences of yesterday. Build a bridge and get over it." Amen to that.

Building the Bridge

So how do we build this bridge? We know there are a number of tried and tested approaches, some of which you'd just read about earlier in this chapter.

Engaging with positive people certainly is a way forward. So too is limiting time with those friends who are notoriously negative and tend to drain your energy. A case for judicious pruning, perhaps?

Simple acts of gratitude and mindfulness in how we spend each day also can make major differences to our outlook and our impact on others. So proudly showcase your attitude of gratitude and pay it forward by being positive and inspiring others around you. You owe it to yourself. Stop and negative thoughts in their tracks and reframe the situation to create positive emotions.

Chapter 8:

Vitality—Lighting a Fire Under Yourself

For an Olympic sprinter, the finish line does not make the end of the race but the spur to crash through it at a pace quicker than the start. Does it sound counter-intuitive? Not if you're Usain Bolt training for the final lunge of the 100-yard dash that often is decided by a photo finish.

It's a sporting analogy that can be compared with the race of life that most of us mortals run. Imagine your life as a lap around the track. You take off like a rocket and put in the hard yards over the first 200 and 300 yards. As we head into the final straight and can see the end winking, you pull up and start slowing down, just as we approach retirement.

It's a short-sighted strategy, both as far as running a race and living life is concerned. A much more productive approach is to hit the finish line at speed and continue running.

In retirement terms, it means you want to maintain your physical activity, live healthy, follow a nutritious diet, and exercise your mind. You're not supposed to slow down but maintain the momentum, even picking up the pace, in your third age.

You're retiring from work, not from life nor living. Imagine yourself competing in the World Retirement Championships; how would you look at your third age differently? Think about the myriad of improvements, in particular making the small changes in your life. You may be surprised at how several small steps make a big difference in the quest for a flourishing retirement.

Yes, it's a tall order. It certainly runs counter to the convention about taking it easy as you enter your golden years. Research has proved, again and again, that you are doing yourself the best favor possible by keeping physically, mentally, and emotionally active.

Health, Happiness, and Quality of Life

Take a closer look at the people radiating warmth and confidence. Odds are they live an active lifestyle because they know that their health and happiness determine their quality of life.

In case it's not clear, their quality of life counts infinitely more than their savings balance. Every moment counts, as does living in the present.

So often we become complacent and take our good health for granted in our late forties and early fifties. And yet, the time leading to your retirement era is probably the most critical period. Instead of adopting the habits and routines to set us up for an active retirement, we do the opposite.

Slowly, almost imperceptibly, we slide into a sedentary life. We sit more and walk less; we eat more and exercise less; we party more and read less.

The world on our mobile phones and computer screens may become larger, but our real world gets smaller. An overload of information forces us into a shrinking bubble of self-preservation that, ironically, hastens our slide into apathy and isolation.

You suffer from less vitality and lower enthusiasm for what matters. We lose our "get-up-and-go" and sink into a morass of numb lethargy and a dull outlook. Nothing really matters. Everything is too much effort. It's all a bit pointless.

Neglecting those critical building blocks of a healthy body and mind come at a cost as we enter our sixties. Our muscles atrophy, bone density declines, and we start losing our physical balance. We start losing confidence in our movement, not to mention the toll on your mental and emotional well-being. It's that simple.

Rowena: Maxing Out on Vitality

Rowena was one determined lady. Well into her seventies, Rowena loved life, sometimes a bit too much. With a passion for the finer things in life, including a love for Italian cuisine and wine, Rowena added a few pounds over the years.

As in most cases of gaining weight, the extra pound here and there did not bother her at first. But gradually the extra load on her body started to take its toll. Over time, the activities she loved like gardening, hiking, and biking became more difficult.

She was losing mobility and range of movement. Getting on her knees for a mulching session or rolling out the bike was more difficult. Slowly, the fun and pleasure of doing what she loved was deserting her.

To be clear, Rowena did not succumb to paralysis. As an active senior with a passion for life, Rowena had been doing functional exercise for too many years to count. She was more mobile, active, and filled with vitality than many of her younger associates.

But Rowena set herself high standards. She knew what she wanted from life and a diminished capacity for doing what made her happy was not part of the deal.

Rowena made two crucial decisions—she took responsibility for her condition and decided to fix things.

Over the next six months, Rowena shed an impressive 33 pounds (15 kg). A sensible diet of more mindful eating was supported by an intense program of exercise that aimed to increase strength and promote flexibility.

Rowena realized a clear vision through hard work. She did some weight lifting under supervision and well within her capabilities and also followed a series of stretching exercises. More impressively, she stepped out of her comfort zone with an energy-sapping program of jumping and skipping.

The results were outstanding. Rowena's sleep quality improved, as did her physical appearance. Most obvious was her increased levels of energy and an energized mood.

Rowena's renewed zest for life was inspiration for some of her friends to follow her example. The small group of ladies soon became the talk of the town as they kept on pushing the boundaries about aging and exercise.

Rowena, and her friends, showed that vitality doesn't happen in a vacuum. Achieving the vigor and energy demands an active decision and followed through by persistent action. The outcome certainly is worth the ride, as Rowena showed. In her own words, "It's not about the weight you lose, it's about the life you gain."

The gains in her life are worth celebrating. Rowena's positivity in taking a stand and turning the tide against her weight and regaining her life through more movement was inspiring. The transformation motivated others as Rowena demonstrated the collective power of small changes in her life.

Soon Rowena was leading a group of women who shared in the pleasure of achieving small wins when they hit yet another intermediate target. Their success became a self-fulfilling prophecy of support, inspiration, action, healthier bodies, happier people, and vibrant vitality. Talk about winning on multiple levels.

Phil: The Folly of Old Habits

Phil was a dear friend who lived an active life of sport and plenty of physical activity. He was in robust health, until he turned 80. It was as if a switch in Phil's head had been flicked—now that I'm 80, it's time to put my feet up and take it slow.

The problem was that his life didn't just slow down; it came to an abrupt stop. The consequences became apparent almost immediately. He started to gain weight rapidly, and that set off a host of ailments, including the onset of type 2 diabetes and cardiovascular troubles.

He soon developed some pains and aches he never had before. His weight-bearing joints started to take strain and, just before his 82nd birthday, was diagnosed with bone-on-bone arthritis. Knee replacement surgery was recommended.

As part of the preoperative preparation, the physiotherapist at our health and wellness practice put Phil on a program of structured exercise. The objective was to cut back on Phil's weight and reduce the load on his knee joints as well as strengthen the muscles around the knees to compensate for the damaged cartilage.

That in turn would promote recovery after his knee replacement surgery.

Calling on the muscle memory of his sporting days, Phil took the therapy to heart and hit the program hard. The results bowled all of us over. Not only did his health improve, but he also gained movement, even in his dodgy knees. The pain receded, and his mobility increased by leaps and bounds. He canceled the surgery.

Perplexing Regression

Five years later, the story read very differently. Phil's prognosis was both heartbreaking and despairing. In short, Phil had reverted to his old, lazy habits. He no longer exercised, and his illnesses returned with a vengeance.

It was a perplexing regression. Phil knew full well that the power to make a difference to his life was in his hands. He even proved the age-old truism to himself!

We tried everything in the book from supporting programs to motivational interventions and more. Not even tearful appeals by his two daughters could sway him.

Truth was that Phil had given up on life. He found the discipline too much and saw no point in giving up on the habits. He shook his head every time his worsening health was brought up and became irritable at our constant reminders.

Sadly, the immediate gratification of eating the wrong food and lounging outweighed the benefits of movement and carrying less weight. In a rare moment of honest reflection, Phil would nod and sigh deeply.

"It's too late to teach an old dog new tricks," he said. "I'm too lazy to put in the effort. I should have kept a tight leash on myself all those years ago."

Phil also acknowledged another saying about learning tricks—that you cannot teach anybody anything unless they're willing to learn or adopt new habits. The reality was that the pain of the present wasn't enough to deal with the promise of a better future. Or as a saying about a whimpering dog refusing to get up goes, "The nail just wasn't sharp enough" (Hanson, 2015).

Getting Real About Aging

We cannot escape the inevitability of aging. But we can limit its consequences. Our modern lifestyles and its emphasis on "creature comforts" have robbed most people of their daily dose of movement, agility, and activity.

The human aging process also strips our bodies of muscle tone, strength, and bone density, particularly among women. These deprivations cause weakness, injury, and restricted range of motion, so much so that you lose confidence in your physical ability.

You start fretting about simple actions like stepping off a pavement, climbing stairs, or negotiating a rocky path.

Over time, the pleasure of rock-hopping makes way for a fear of tripping, slipping, or falling and a painful injury.

Sadly, the more nervous you become, the more restrictions you impose on yourself. You tell yourself, "I don't want to fall. At my age, I need to be careful."

There's wisdom in assessing the risk of injury. Recognize your physical limitations and pay heed to legitimate concerns as recklessness seldomly ends well.

Not All Is Lost, Far From It

It's surprising how many seniors fall victim to the fears of aging. Often, the biggest challenge is making them see the wood for the trees, that the loss of your physical attributes doesn't sound the death knell.

There's plenty of evidence about how muscle memory helps your body to fight aging through regular and structured movement. The key to active aging is a disarmingly simple solution—a positive mindset to build happy habits and, very importantly, to establish your own routine.

An early-morning routine not only primes your body for the day ahead, it also offers its own reward. You've already taken the first step to make your day and your life better. Take it a step further with an exercise routine of 15-30 minutes that will add lasting benefits.

Take Courage

The importance of personalizing your own routine, of finding your own groove, cannot be overstated. In my experience, one of the biggest obstacles to a successful activity program is slavishly following others. Don't get me wrong; inspiration from others is good, but imitation not so much.

Not all inspiring ideas are always the perfect fit for you or anybody else. So much depends on your special circumstances, your targets, even who you are. It's not quite shooting in the dark for answers but close enough.

Be wary of claims that a single diet, or a specific supplement, will improve, if not cure, a condition. Rarely, in our experience, did one isolated intervention make a meaningful difference. A considered response that covers all the bases did. Diet and exercise, for example, go together in the same way that nutrition and movement do.

Finding your balance is key. You may need to experiment with diets and see what works for you. It may come down to when you eat or even when you exercise.

On the Move

Trawl cyberspace for ideas, beliefs, and the things people get up to. Treat these as morsels of inspiration and instead consult with credible sources that are certifiably science-backed.

By all means, talk to friends and family for referrals. If you're planning major changes to your exercise and nutrition habits, consult with your primary care physician first, and then talk with some allied professionals.

Consider Pilates, Tai Chi, yoga, and the like to re-introduce your body to movement patterns it may have forgotten. Find local trainers, walking guides, groups, and like-minded people who are already on the move. Test the waters and join them to see what a difference small changes will make.

Listen to your body and take things relatively slowly if you are starting from a low activity base.

There's plenty of inspiration from nature, not least the popularity of an early-morning exercise session among seniors. Not only do you greet the sun as it rises, but early morning exercise also firms up your activity goals for the day (Terrace, 2016).

Nutrition, Nutrition, Nutrition

"You are what you eat" is a well-worn adage that pretty much speaks for itself. The quote dates back to a time of stress in 1848 during a revolution in Germany, but its meaning has not changed over the past 175 years (Cizza and Rother, 2011).

The importance of quality sleep cannot be overstated and is sometimes regarded as the seventh essential nutrient, along with the traditional six nutrients:

- protein

- carbohydrates

- fats

- vitamins

- minerals

- water

There's general scientific consensus that natural, untainted foods provide the best quality nutrition. A push-back against processed foods that contain artificial preservatives has elevated the role of organic produce.

There's no doubt that unprocessed food and a reduced sugar intake as part of a moderate consumption of calories will bring about a positive change in how you feel. Who knows, you may even rediscover the joys of cooking from first principles again.

We're fortunate to have the space and climate to grow most of our vegetables and fruit. We also source other produce locally from organic stores and farmers markets. We also barter, or swap, excess produce with our neighbors. Sharing is indeed caring.

On that score, a small amount of home-brewed alcohol tends to wash down produce most agreeably and has been known to influence a buying decision on occasion.

Otherwise, we recommend you scrutinize the labels on bottles and canned food for additives you'd rather do without. Overall, be more mindful about what you are consuming and preparing. It's the fuel for your body, so treat it with the care and respect it deserves.

A Personal Account

Around the age of 50, I noticed a seismic shift in the health of friends and colleagues. We're all part, more or less, of the same age cohort, but somehow the great majority of fellow nine-to-fivers seemed to complain non-stop about all sorts of illnesses and ailments.

Some were diagnosed with hypertension and coronary heart disease, others with early-stage diabetes, most of them overweight and obese. Others grumbled about their aches and pains and the cost of physio to sort out a hurt back or a stiff neck. They were, for the most part, a sorry lot who were genuinely sick, lame, or lazy.

I sometimes had to bite my tongue not to be critical of their choices. Exercise and being fit was important to me, especially after a competitive athletic career. I had transitioned into coaching and adopted regular gym and swimming routines. Thankfully, I had escaped the chorus of moans and groans apart from the effects of a few sporting injuries. I now pay particular attention to these "combat wounds" to maintain my mobility and flexibility as well as stability in my movements.

The disgruntled choir did plant a seed in my subconsciousness though. I woke up one morning knowing what I'd wanted to do: learn everything more about the body, its health, and aging.

Building from my passion for physical training and exercise, I qualified as a Master PTI with a few areas of interest, notably kettlebell and boxing as exercise options.

My sights were set firmly on the future. Retirement was coming, and I wanted to be skilled enough to help my peers and others who were not aging well to transition the best they could.

Subtle Lane Change

My change in approach opened doors I had not anticipated. I learned, for example, the nuances of personal training, the subtleties of giving people instructions so that they feel good about exercise and what it brings to their lives.

More importantly, it helped me to train, guide, and assist people who had never thought about exercising with a PTI or in a gym. They proved that you're never too old to learn something new for the first time. It also improved the quality of their lives on a daily basis. Like

Rowena, they're discovering that the changes are more about what they gain than what they lose.

They found that they had greater physical strength to load and carry groceries. They could also get in and out of a car or chair more easily and had more cardio and aerobic ability to enjoy hiking, riding, kayaking, or walking.

They also moved with more balance, coordination, and confidence and felt less vulnerable to falls, tripping, and slipping.

They experienced greater mental focus and health and had a great self-care start to the day that set a purposeful and positive tone for the day ahead.

Final Words

Set some small goals. Adopt a structured plan to ensure you stick to it and kick start your revitalization. Think about why you're wanting to make changes. Picture the vitality you'll gain. Be confident about your ability.

Learn from a trained professional who will tailor a program to your physical needs and limitations. They will also factor in likes and lifestyle.

Find your tribe. Join a group of like-minded people. You should get the physical benefits of exercise as well as draw on the company and support of a group or buddy to keep you motivated.

Find like-minded others by joining a walking group, yoga circle, or Tai Chi class.

Look out for specialist groups catering to mature clients, be it for physical or mental exercise needs.

Start small and build on your options and other fun ways to exercise as your ability strengthens.

Do something positive at the start of every day. The small ritual will set you up for a long and active game in life.

Identify what you like to do but are not able to. Ask yourself the following:

- What is holding you back?

- What do you need to start doing?

- What do you need to do more of?

- What do you need to stop doing?

Take stock of what you're consuming. Cut down on the processed foods with its additives and preservatives. Also limit the amount of sugar and alcohol.

Just do it, start doing something, anything, today. Take the first step, the others will follow. Stepping out will become easier each day, just as your confidence and capability does.

Chapter 9:

Finances, Not

This chapter is clearly not about doling out financial advice. There are specialists for that. We do, however, recognize that a degree of financial security is important to most of us. It gives us greater freedom in what we choose to do and how we pursue those goals.

It's important to work out what you will need for the retirement lifestyle you are planning. Do it in collaboration with your partner, family, and your financial advisor. Starting this planning phase early hopefully means you'll have made some great decisions and investments. It will give you comfort and clarity in what you can achieve before you retire and when you do retire.

Fearing the Future

Being fearful about not having enough financial resources for retirement is perfectly normal. We're weighed down by a raft of worries—how will we continue to live the lifestyle we're accustomed to, will we have enough to cater for our increasing longevity, how will we fund our travel plans, the list goes on.

Fears about finances is a key factor that stops many seniors from leaving behind the workforce and entering the retirement phase of life. But it needn't be.

Action, particularly action focused on establishing clear goals with your advisor, is the best remedy. And remember—transitioning through part-time or contract work provides a realistic option. Not only does a compromise route address several practical concerns, it also buys you time while you refine your retirement plan.

Don't lose sight of the inalienable truth that the longer you defer your decision to retire, the less time you'll have to enjoy retirement. The peace of mind you, like me, can get from a planned and managed retirement is what we're aiming for. Consider what money can give you as well as what it can't.

Happiness is arguably humankind's most valuable commodity, even if we can't measure it in tangible terms. We know the joy of happiness because we have experienced its feel-good high in the short term. Longer term, happiness is more of a state of mind, of contentment in whatever situation you find yourself in.

Happiness is a universal quality but measured subjectively. Happiness means different things to people. For some, happiness is a state of mind money can't buy.

The tiny Himalayan nation of Bhutan pioneered the Gross National Happiness (GNH) index built on the pillars of

- sustainable and equitable socio-economic development

- environmental conservation

- preservation and promotion of culture

- good governance.

The Bhutan GNH has its critics, but its focus on reflective contentment keeps on resonating across the world. The ethos of simplicity has special significance for people on the cusp of retiring.

Focus on Simplicity

It's deeply significant that Dr. Seligman's thoughts on flourishing and the key factors in his PERMA-V model, does not include finances. The focus instead is on Positive Emotions, Engagement, Relationships, creating Meaning or purpose, an ongoing sense of Achievement and growth, as well as self-care and Vitality.

In other words, we can flourish in a simpler, less expensive lifestyle instead of treading the mill at work and powering the rat race.

The simple-living ethos in retirement is an important but often overlooked option among seniors. The pursuit of a spiritual happiness sets the philosophy apart from the unrelenting focus on wealth and materialism in planning for the golden era.

It challenges the age-old fallacy—that a successful retirement equates to monetary wealth, opulent living, and ostentatious displays of privilege.

For some, the trappings of materialism are very important. It's evident where they live, how they live, how they show off. The thrill of immediate gratification needs more of the same, a relentless compulsion. And that's okay if it is an active choice and important to them about who they are. Just don't stumble into a pothole accidentally.

For others, the third age is a time of adventure and living experiences that no amount of money can buy. If that's hard to think of, imagine each passing day as time that's gone from your life. Be present for every moment and consciously decide how you are spending the precious commodity of time.

There's nothing morbid about it. It's the passing of a precious commodity, just like the other precious commodities—-purpose, connection, love, energy, health, and happiness. They also pass and with it an opportunity to seek out these moments of personal magic.

These alternative currencies are way too valuable to be counted in dollars and cents. How do you possibly monetize life, what you bring to the world, or the difference you make in other people's lives?

Learn to count your wealth in the value of alternative currencies. Money is the means to an end, not the end itself. See it for what it is and deploy it with purpose and mindfulness. Don't let money stop you from living your life as if it's your last moment on Earth.

Take the old story many of us have heard in various iterations. The message is simple yet clear.

Lesson in Island Paradise

A wealthy businessman on vacation to a tropical paradise was watching a group of islanders horsing around where the waves gently rolled onto the beach. A few were fishing off the rocks. Behind them, on a small rise overlooking the beach, bamboo dwellings on stilts stood out against the verdant tropical greenery.

He turned to his friend. "Can you believe it? Look at those lazy fellows cavorting as if they've no cares in the world."

"What's wrong with what they're doing?" his friend asked.

"What do you mean? They should be working hard, saving so they can buy a decent house, car, and everything else they want."

"I see. So what do you want to do when you stop working?"

"Oh, that's easy," he said. "I'll have a house by the beach so I can go fishing every day and not have a worry in the world."

His friend nodded at the frolicking people on the beach.

"Sounds like you want what those people already have."

The hypocrisy was lost on the businessman. Blinded by wealth and privilege, the businessman ranted against the very same values he was aspiring to. His confused sense of entitlement clouded his judgment about what he really wanted out of life. The focus was on what he didn't have yet, not what he had already.

Clear Your Head

Time is money, so be clear in your mind about what you want from retirement. If finances are a concern, figure out your exact needs and budget accordingly. Work out what is 'enough' to have the life you want.

By all means talk to a trusted financial advisor. Hopefully common sense will prevail, and you will be able to differentiate between legitimate expenses— housing, food, medical costs—and nice-to-haves like entertainment, dining, and expensive holidays.

Get into the habit of investigating all the options before spending on a big-ticket item. Think about what you want and why you want it. Will it improve your life and make you happier? Often it will, and at other times, it might seem like an impulsive desire or misguided wish for immediate gratification.

A big ticket item could be a new energy-efficient stove, a lounge suite, or traveling to an exotic destination. You may be surprised how appropriate and cost-effective pausing and checking your actual needs can be. The same applies to undertaking sound research.

The Power of Quality Over Quantity

Much as we all need money to survive, it should not be your overriding focus in the lead up to retirement. Do the sums, prioritize your needs and wants, and discuss these with your financial advisor.

You will arrive at a more sustainable position if you focus on the quality of time and ways to thrive than the quantity of money.

Remember, you have options within the retirement space. If having read this far into the book and the thought of a blank day ahead with nothing to do fills you with anxiety, the answer may be a part-time job or a gentler transition to retirement.

Don't forget to appreciate and enjoy the extra free time in your week. Find your joy, explore different activities, live those extra moments away from work knowing you still have the safety net of an income. Best of all, the move will give you a sense of purpose as well as giving you the time to explore, play, and find your happy life

Remember to pause, reflect, and think about what you really need. Set out to experience those things that bring the greatest joy and fulfillment, what money generally cannot buy.

It's your life—live it and love the outcomes.

Chapter 10:

Fun, Joy, and Soul—Don't Forget To Pack a Smile

"Life is short—smile while you still have teeth." Anon.

Hopefully the quote was enough of a reminder to move you on from the previous chapter and awaken your desire to be truly happy. You want to enjoy your life and find beauty in the small but often powerful everyday events ahead of you. You are responsible for your happiness, but don't overthink it.

Sometimes people try so hard to be happy, they forget to have fun. They do all the right things but with no spontaneity and passion. They tend to take life very seriously and don't know how to have fun. Sometimes having fun is far too frivolous for serious people like them.

We, on the other hand, believe there's nothing better than lots of fun and loads of laughter. We need joy in our lives, the laughter and warmth it brings. We must be able to laugh, or at least have a chuckle, at life and its foibles, especially at our own expense.

As Mark Twain said, "Never regret anything that made you smile."

Life can be harsh at times, even unfair. We deal with life-changing events differently. Often the difference is in how we think about it and asking ourselves what lessons we take from the experience.

The work of American philosopher Ralph Waldo Trine supports the perspective. "To get up each morning with the resolve to be happy is to set our own conditions to the events of each day. To do this is to condition circumstances rather than be conditioned by them."

In short, own your choices and actions and include your mood.

There's truth behind the saying that "laughter is the best medicine"; it's a well-documented scientific principle based on the positive emotions of amusement, happiness, mirth, and joy that increase well-being and life satisfaction.

Laughter also builds resilience and reduces stress. It strengthens the immune system and lifts the mood. What is there not to like about laughter?

The scientific evidence says happiness and laughter is good for our health. Even better is that laughter lifts every moment and lightens every action. Besides, having a happy laugh is a much better bet than drowning in a miserable morass of grumpiness.

Fear of Letting Go, or At Least Relaxing a Little

Strange as it sounds, but some people actually are fearful of having fun. The reluctance may be due to several reasons, including negative experiences in the past. You may feel intimidated or vulnerable or don't want to risk rejection.

The downside is that you deny yourself the chance of pleasure, almost at any cost. Learn to relax, "go with the flow," and talk to other people. You may be surprised at how much fun it can be.

Remind yourself that having fun starts with you. You set the tone and must decide if you want to shun or embrace a new experience. Remember that our past performance doesn't determine our future… unless we let it. The onus is on to create the positive future we desire. Start with simple things like a smile and positive intentions.

"Use your smile to change the world but don't let the world change your smile." Unknown

Our thoughts shape our ability and willingness to have fun and enjoy life. And don't take yourself too seriously.

As Henry Ford said, "If you think you can do a thing, or you think you can't do a thing, you're always right."

Harry: Lifetime of Happiness

Some people have a rare gift of lightening up a room when they enter it. They command more than a presence but radiate a lightness of being.

My friend Harry is one of those people. And yet there was nothing outwardly special about him. He had an ordinary physique, was of average height, and was no great shakes in the looks department.

In fact, he was a good 10 years older than me. But there was something about Harry and the positivity he projected. He certainly was not swimming in money, and part of Harry's allure was his non-materialistic humility.

We met through mutual acquaintances, and I was struck by his *joie de vie*, an exuberant enjoyment of life. I've never seen Harry with a scowl or even a troubled look on his face. If he didn't beam a benevolent smile, he would be chuckling or laughing out loud about something.

Harry was a wonderful storyteller with fine observational powers. The funniest stories were about his misadventures or those at his expense. He would find the humor in whatever story or misadventure he related.

Not a word of malice of anger would cross his lips. He would gently steer the conversation away from contentious topics and criticism of other people, often through humor.

It was difficult not to like Harry. Not even his deteriorating health could get him down.

We spent many wonderful hours together over our shared passion for food and wine. Those memorable hours were filled with laughter but also the lessons of life. Over time, I realized that Harry's life was a template for achieving genuine joy in life. This is what I came up with.

Bright Side of Life

Harry had a knack for always looking at the bright side of life. He gave true expression to words from the comedy song by Monty Python member Eric Idle and duly featured in the cult film, *Life of Brian*.

The lesson from Harry we can apply to our lives is quite simple. It's about reframing our stories and looking for the joy that sneaks in... when we let it.

Ode to Joy

We all deserve fun and joy in our lives. That's the reward for the serious business of living. Challenges and difficulties are the facts of life, and it's up to us to find the enjoyment and joy that makes life worth living. We're not talking non-stop partying till you fall over; just a sober statement of joyous intent.

In the words of Aeschylus, "Happiness is a choice that requires effort at times." He had it right, so make the effort and craft your own rewards.

Make the Most

Do an audit about life and your precious alternative currencies. Now transpose these qualities on a time graph. See how much time you have left to do what you've always wanted.

Hopefully you have more time than you think. Remind yourself of all the positive opportunities out there waiting for you. Ask yourself how to make the most of them.

Live for every moment. Let each moment be purposeful. Find calm joy in yourself. Be grateful for what you have. Be gracious in your contentment and wear your smile with pride. Know that life is joyous, even if you have made a mistake or two along the way. Fun is there to be had. You've just got to find it.

No Regrets

Life is too short for regrets. Look forward in anticipation, not back with regrets. Instead, view those unfortunate incidents and episodes as "life lessons not to be repeated."

As James M. Barrie said, "The secret of happiness is not in doing what one likes but in liking what one does."

Forget about regrets—you cannot change them. Focus on the immediate life you can impact.

Living for Now

Live life in the present. The past is for memories, and the future are dreams still to come true. But there's no better time to live than today and making each moment count.

A mindful approach to everything we do, everything we choose, and being present in the moment to see the beauty around us can be one of the most empowering ways to create a life filled with happiness and fulfillment. The power is in the simplicity of doing this.

Open Mind

Be willing to experiment or try something new. As the popular adage goes, "When's the last time you tried something for the first time?" Being receptive to a new adventure, or meeting people, is key. Only once we open our minds can we take pleasure in the unexpected.

Take a chance and check out what some of your more adventurous friends and acquaintances are up to. Find what gives them pleasure and adds spark to their lives.

Positive People

By surrounding yourself with positive people, you absorb their energy and "can do" attitude. People who radiate that kind of zest often bring pleasure and happiness to other people.

"Spend your life with people who make you smile, laugh, and feel loved." So said Roy T. Bennett, author of *The Light in the Heart*, who understood the power of positive impact.

To make the most of time with positive people, you may need to make room by cutting out, or limiting as diplomatically as possible, time with people who don't fit into your world view or who don't bring you pleasure. Don't allow others to drag you down; there's too much to be grateful for.

Seeing Is Believing

Beauty is all around us, but we often are blind to it. Some people are threatened by what they don't know and choose to stay in the dark.

The reality is that as we age, we start limiting our choices and experiences. Our world starts to shrink, and our microcosmic existence becomes our life at the exclusion of what's really happening around us. We only see what we allow ourselves to see.

Sometimes you need to remove the scales from your eyes to see things for what they are. Wanting to see clearly is a choice, as much as homing in on a vision for yourself.

Choose to see and explore the wonders around you. Start small if you have forgotten how. Explore your neighborhood again and don't overlook the park. If you need help, rope in a friend who has their eyes wide open to the wonders of every day. See what's in front of you, find inspiration, and enjoy the simple pleasures around you. They may even make you smile, making someone else's day as well.

Laugh Out Loud

Inspired as I am by Harry and his love for life, I am not Harry. I express my emotions differently, my circumstances are unique, and I live life the way it makes me happy. There is no wrong or right, it's what works for you. It's about finding your groove.

A final word about the healing power of laughter. Some people have more reason to laugh than say Harry. But they don't, for whatever reason. But when they do give themselves over to mirth, and they giggle, guffaw, and chortle, they bring as much light to a room and joy to people as Harry. That in itself is worth a chuckle.

What you choose is a matter of choice, your choice. You're not going to find happiness or your groove if you're not looking. Start now. Find a reason to smile or laugh at the funny side of life.

Check and Reflect

When all is said and done, and we're reflecting on the purpose of life, the joy of living is right up there. Otherwise, why are we here in the first place? We've all tasted the pleasure of deep happiness that surely is one of the most persuasive reasons for seeking playful outlets.

How you choose to have fun is up to you because everybody is different. But we're not split on the need to pursue joy hard and fast, or slow and leisurely.

Here are some reminders to help you in your pursuit:

- People and activities bring you joy. They leave you richer and happier for the experience. Connect with positive people, build meaningful relationships, do more of those activities that bring meaning or fulfillment to your day.

- Cull what is dragging you down. A miserable narcissist who drains your energy, a toxic friendship, or a bad job are examples of things to expunge. Allow yourself more opportunities to engage in activities that bring pleasure and a sense of achievement.

- Live for now. The past is for remembering, the future is for dreaming, and the present is for living. Enough said.

- Stride out and do what you want to do. Coffee and cake over a chat? A solitary stroll to check out the lilies in the forest? A Zoom call to your child on a different continent? Seize the moment, own the experience.

- Adopt an attitude with purpose. Your attitude and path forward will impact others. Think of the likely consequences. What would you prefer to happen? How could you make that work?

Go out and enjoy life!

Conclusion

All roads lead to retirement. After a life of hopefully gainful employment, we're heading for the third age of our lives. It's a simple truth we cannot escape. The second inescapable truth is that destiny—your retirement—is in your hands.

Time is precious, and no doubt you're looking forward to a lengthy and fruitful retirement. That surely is the strongest reason to design your retirement to suit you.

We all aspire to be healthy and mobile to do what we enjoy. Key to those goals are a positive mental attitude and desire to enjoy life to the maximum. Joining in pleasurable and rewarding activities with your friends, old and new, gives special meaning to those simple things that help us find greater purpose in all things big and small that we purposefully participate in.

The quest for a fulfilling retirement is the central theme of this book. We've approached retirement from a quality of life perspective. That's why we advocate alternative currencies to gauge the intangible qualities of our lives—those attributes we cannot wish back once they're gone.

Nothing is more precious than time, as is your health, purposefulness, love, and happiness. These qualities money can't buy, but you hold the power to invest in these currencies for your retirement.

Retirement Is Not a Spectator Sport

The finger points to you and your choices. Retirement is not a spectator sport; it demands your active involvement.

You want to avoid an unplanned or forced retirement at all costs. Thinking about what you want, and your options, is a good starting point. Take your time. You've been working for the most part of your life, and there's no need to rush into a course of action for your third age. Make it an active, mindful, and purposeful process. Write down and prioritize your ideas and how doable they are in retirement.

An enduring myth is that you only retire from something, like work. But you also should retire to something that you want for yourself and your life. It's surprising how many people don't know who they are or what they want to do. Remember, don't let the uncertainty stop you. Don't procrastinate; chase it, start exploring, test different ideas, dip your toes in new waters.

Refine and work with the concepts that bring pleasure and satisfaction, and yes, that includes those notions that challenge you. Drawing up a rough plan and acting on it with a sense of excitement about the potential is a critical early step.

Once you've settled on a course of action, the hard part is putting those wishes and desires into practice. Often, it requires tough decisions and disciplined action to make the changes happen. You may have to let go of some things that are comfortable in order to move forward. Embrace change and the opportunities it can bring.

Still, and no matter how well you prepare, the best-laid plans sometimes are upended. A Plan B and flexibility in your planning will limit some of the disruptions. A positive attitude, however, will build resilience to deal with hidden ambushes.

Purposeful Change

Making purposeful changes in your life also requires fortitude. Often, taking small steps in the desired direction is the best way forward because it allows you to test the waters. And remember it's a journey where you can always make adjustments. You're not locked in. You are regularly exploring new opportunities and ideas. You are constantly trying them out, testing them, reflecting, and refining them on your quest for the best retirement possible.

Don't forget the reason for retirement in the first place—happiness and fulfillment. It's easy to lose focus of what really matters and be overwhelmed or distracted by the myriad of options out there.

Make sure what you do actually aligns with your values and principles as well as your likes and wants. Find like-minded people and engage in activities that build social capital and a sense of gratitude for having found your space and place in time.

However, if you're not getting what you need from what you're doing, it's probably a signal to rethink, or refine, your ideas. Changing a plan is not failure; it's an astute response to the realities of life. Your plan and your life will be better for it.

With more time on your hands, you'll be able to pursue the passions you weren't able to before. Check out other interests too, like volunteering or contributing to a community or church endeavor. These activities add meaning and purpose to our lives and are cited as the most important reason for a happy retirement.

To Flourish

Happiness cannot be measured in tangible terms, but Dr. Seligman's framework of happiness does a fine job of describing it. At the center of the iconic PERMA-V model is the notion of 'flourishing,' of living life to the fullest.

It's fitting that we revisit the model at the conclusion of the book.

Positivity (Positive Emotions)

As Brian of Monty Python lore said, "Always look on the bright side of life." Be optimistic about what's ahead. Be happy with who you are and what you have, and stop wasting time wishing for something else or something different. Strive to be the best you can be.

By creating and sharing positive emotions such as optimism, gratitude, happiness, and serenity, you will promote resilience, inspiration, and cheerfulness. I'm sure we can all do with more of that.

Engagement (Being in the Present 100%)

Being in the present could be as simple as reading for understanding and enjoyment. Or breathing in the smells and listening to the sounds when you walk in the wilderness with your mind 100% engrossed in the experience. Or being in your "flow state" during your special, passionate activity where time disappears as you are swept along by the experience.

I know that I certainly lose track of time when I'm cruising down hill on my mountain bike, managing the turns, jumps, and climbs, albeit a tad more slowly than my more youthful counterparts.

Relationships (People Who Really Matter)

They may challenge you to be your real and authentic self, and they make you—and your life—better for it. You know who I mean... those trusted supportive friends and family who are there for you and each other. They don't tolerate your nonsense and help you to be the best version of yourself and take pleasure from the relationship. Don't lose that. Build on it and grow it more.

Meaning (In Life, of Life)

Meaning is often positioned as a belief that your actions or behavior matters to people other than yourself. It is also linked to a bigger cause, but I don't think that's necessary as long as you see your efforts contributing to something other than just filling your time. For me, part of this is as simple as transforming a landscape on our property creatively and positively.

Finding meaning is as simple as spending time on activities that give you fulfillment and seem worthwhile. Helping others often comes into this but is not essential. What are yours?

Achievement (Celebrating Success)

We can all relate to the elation of completing or accomplishing a challenging task. It's a "Wow... I did it!" feeling when you succeed with something tough or beyond your normal skills. It's a special feeling of success or winning at something you weren't good at when you started.

Often it's about hitting personal milestones—fitness, weight loss, golf handicap, and so forth—that we achieve through dedicated and focused effort.

Vitality (Brimming with Life's Essence)

Vitality is a special quality that radiates the positive essence energy and enthusiasm for all things. We all know or have met someone who demonstrates this. They are truly 'alive,' and every moment is a precious gem to be savored.

There is no room for a "glass half full" mentality here. It's a physical as well as mental state of well-being that puts the power of your actions in your reach. I'm pretty sure vitality is the result of living the first five PERMA qualities well.

Practice the PERMA-V mantra, and before you know it, you'll be envied as "one of those people" who are always bubbly and brimming with energy.

Throughout the book, we've reflected and looked at some of the lessons I have witnessed and mostly learned from. Remember, the adventures we live are the experiences that bring us life.

It's your life. Make the most of your retirement. I wish you a life as rich or richer than mine. May it be filled with wonder and daily pleasures.

Go out there and retire. Do it your way. Be strong in your conviction that you'll make it work for you. You are in the driver's seat.

Put pedal to metal and enjoy the ride of your life.

About the Author

Ramon knows about retirement. He's living it and has seen a cross section of successes and failures up close.

Ramon retired early at age 57 from a career spanning Communication, Product Development, Strategy and Business Consultancy. He is passionate about wellness and positive psychology which compliment his Master Trainer qualifications.

Early into retirement Ramon was thrown a curve ball – via a serious spinal condition challenging his mobility and almost derailing his retirement dreams. His training and ongoing education in mental, emotional and physical well-being became critical to his recovery and ability to keep the dream alive.

Ramon and his wife continue to live on acreage in the Sunshine Coast of Australia where they are both active in the community and enjoy the hiking, bike riding and canoeing opportunities that abound in this area.

References

50 Inspiring gratitude quotes. (2017). Ideas and inspiration for every occasion. *Shutterfly*. www.shutterfly.com/ideas/gratitude-quotes/.

Ackerman, C. (2019). What is positive psychology & why is it important? *PositivePsychology.com*. www.positivepsychology.com/what-is-positive-psychology-definition/.

Branch, M. (2015). Inspiring Eleanor Roosevelt quotes. *Unfoundation.org*. www.unfoundation.org/blog/post/10-inspiring-eleanor-roosevelt-quotes/.

Cherry, K. (2019) Why our brains are hardwired to focus on the negative. *Verywell Mind*. www.verywellmind.com/negative-bias-4589618.

Cizza, G & Rother, K. (2011) Was Feuerbach right: Are we what we eat? *The Journal of Clinical Investigation*, 121, 8, 2969–2971. www.ncbi.nlm.nih.gov/pmc/articles/PMC3148750/.

Colvin, K. (2015) The three stages of gratitude. *Pacifica Psychological Services*. www.kathlinecolvin.com/the-three-stages-of-gratitude/.

Cote, C. (2022). Growth mindset vs. fixed mindset: What's the difference? *Business Insights Blog*.

online.hbs.edu/blog/post/growth-mindset-vs-fixed-mindset.

Crowfoot, T. (2022). What are the secrets to a long, healthy life? 10 Stories to Read. *World Economic Forum.* www.weforum.org/agenda/2022/11/live-longer-healthier-life-stories-to-read/.

Hanson, C. (2015). Money mission: Discover your motivating force. *Financially S.M.A.R.T. Advice.* www. financiallysmartadvice.com/money-mission-discover-your-motivating-force/.

Hoyt, J. (2022). Top 10 fears of older adults in 2022. *SeniorLiving.org.* www.seniorliving.org/finance/senior-fears-study/.

Maestas, N. (2010). Back to work: Expectations and realizations of work after retirement. *Journal of Human Resources,* 45, 3, 718–748, 10.1353/jhr.2010.0011.

Oppong, T. (2019) Good social relationships are the most consistent predictor of a happy life. *The Center for Compassion and Altruism Research and Education.* www.ccare.stanford.edu/press_posts/good-social-relationships-are-the-most-consistent-predictor-of-a-happy-life/.

Ortiz-Ospina, E & Roser, M. (2020). Loneliness and social connections. *Our World in Data.* www. ourworldindata.org/social-connections-and-loneliness.

Quarterly Retirement Market Data, Second Quarter 2022. (2022). *Investment Company Institute.* www.ici.org/statistical-report/ret_22_q2.

Quotes Falsely Attributed to Winston Churchill. (2008). *The International Churchill Society.* www.winstonchurchill.org/resources/quotes/quotes-falsely-attributed/.

Seligman, et al. (2005). Positive psychology progress: Empirical validation of interventions. *Psycnet.apa.org.* www.psycnet.apa.org/record/2005-08033-003.

Terrace, D. (2016). Rise and shine: The benefits of early morning exercise for older adults. *Umh.org.* www.umh.org/assisted-independent-living-blog/rise-and-shine-the-benefits-of-early-morning-exercise-for-older-adults.

Trott, K. (2018). Untreated hearing loss can lead to dementia - Westender. *Westender Community News.* www.westender.com.au/untreated-hearing-loss-can-lead-dementia/.

Vandenbroucke, G. (2019). How many people will be retiring in the years to come? *Stlouisfed.org.* www.stlouisfed.org/on-the-economy/2019/may/how-many-people-will-be-retiring-in-the-years-to-come.

Yim, J. (2016) Therapeutic benefits of laughter in mental health: A theoretical review. *The Tohoku Journal of Experimental Medicine*, 239, 3, 243–249. www.jstage.jst.go.jp/article/tjem/239/3/239_243.

Made in the USA
Coppell, TX
29 November 2023